The

MINDCHEMIST

QUIETING THE MIND:
SET YOUR MIND FREE AND DISCOVER FOR YOURSELF.

BY

PAUL GHATTAS

The
MindChemist

To request permission, contact the publisher at
info@themindchemist.com

ISBN: 978-1-7773600-1-6 (Paperback)
ISBN: 978-1-7773600-2-3 (Ebook)

Edited by: Tahlia Newland
Cover art by: Paul Ghattas
Layout Design by: Paul Ghattas

First paperback edition December 2020
Published by Paul Ghattas
www.themindchemist.com

I am humbled and grateful for this human experience. My deepest gratitude goes to those who have listened to me without judgment, and held my hand and guided me, without entitlement.
I dedicate this book to you, and to:
My ancestors and my guides,
My family and my friends,
Mother Earth and the Amazonian jungle,
S.N.Goenka (1924-2013).

Contents

PROLOGUE

Life is an adventure, and that's an understatement. I am continuously humbled on this journey I find myself on. In 2009 my entire reality shifted, but I didn't feel a wave of change take place from within until 2016. What is this wave I'm talking about? I can't slap a label on it, nor do I wish to label it. It was energetic in nature, that's all I can tell you for now. The fog will clear as you go through this book. The shift that started in 2016, continued throughout 2017, and up until the first half of 2018.

Don't get me wrong, the shift didn't stop; it's still going on right now, even at the time of releasing this book (2020). The reason why I said 'Up until the first half of 2018' was because during that time period, the intensity of this wave significantly increased, and it reached a point where it was too potent for me to be able to simply ignore and power through it. I felt that I couldn't do anything other than give in and let go.

You may be thinking, what is this change he's talking about? What does he mean by give in and let go? Give in to what? And let go of what exactly? I let go of the way I used to see life, and the way I understood life. I let go of all the stories I was told. I let go of my dream life, or at least what I thought had been my dream life at the time.

From there I traveled from one city to another, from one country to another, exposing myself to different frequencies, cultures, traditions and beliefs. Simply following my inner guidance without questioning it. I went through many challenges that I would later appreciate. Some I share with you in this book. It wasn't too long after that day when I let go that I realized there was much more to this reality–much more to what I was experiencing at the time.

The 2018 wave time period set me on a road that led to the writing of this book. What happened in 2018 exactly? What was the catalyst that got me going? I can trace it back to one night. It all happened fast. It was sudden. I had no notice and no forewarning. It was a Thursday night. I had just taken a hot shower after a long day at work, followed by a yoga (asana) class which was followed by a soccer game. I then found myself lying down on my couch with my eyes closed. I can't put what happened next into words, but I'll do my best. I began to feel the presence of some sort of invisible cushion next to me. It was very soft and very gentle. Next thing I know, I start to connect dots between experiences that I had back in 2009, roughly nine years previous, and then I was shown images of myself just walking around the house doing the same thing again and again. It was as if this cushion was making fun me.

The first question I had at the time was, what is this cushion? I then thought to myself, maybe I should be asking who is this cushion? I wanted to know who was sending me those images? And why were they showing me those specific images? What was I supposed to do with them? Was I supposed to interpret them and learn from them? I made a quick decision to write down what I saw, then I simply went to bed. That night triggered a series of events that I cannot necessarily address through logic alone.

I found myself tuning into people and giving them messages that literally just came through. It truly felt like a game. It started off with someone (an old friend) popping into my mind, and I began to feel them–without knowing I was doing so at the time. When I say I felt them, I mean I actually felt whatever it was they were going through. I then followed my instinct to call them (which generally I wouldn't have done) even if they were in another country. We'd start the conversation, and then one thing would lead to another, and then suddenly they're either crying or completely silent on the phone. The theme was always the same. They'd say, "How did you know that's what I needed to hear?" Or, "I was just praying to get more clarity with regards to my situation, and here you are, giving me just that, as if you heard me."

At that time I was still trying to make sense of it myself. In the beginning my answer to them was always the same: "I have no clue how I knew. I simply felt it and then I acted on it. I don't 'think' about what I'm saying; I simply 'speak' and whatever comes through, comes through. It all just happens. I, too, feel like a witness of this experience."

Patience was never my strong suit. But I noticed that I had become even more impatient around that period, and it would take a while before I figured out why. It's because when I'm having a conversation with someone, a few minutes into the conversation, I already know what that person is about to tell me, or the response that they are thinking about, based on what I've just said to them. And because I'm in tune with their thoughts (unconsciously) I found myself interrupting them, because I already had the conversation, I was about to have with them in my head. So when we actually enacted it in physical form, it felt as if there was a lag, some sort of latency. It's like the world outside of me is very slow and it's catching up with me.

Suddenly, I had zero tolerance to small talk. I (my intellect) had no clue that was the case until later on. I learned how to be patient and compassionate to my mind, and to my body, as I observed their habit patterns, and slowly I guided them without judgement and without force.

This rollercoaster has been humbling, fun and exciting in many ways.

I later learned that what happens is this: The pieces of the puzzle only come together as you continue on the path. With every step you take, you'll find another piece which will lead you to your next step. We're not meant to know what's beyond our next step. All we need to do is to take that step in the present moment. That's one of the biggest challenges we face. We want to know the destination and control this so-called future. This concept will become clearer later in the book.

Along this journey, my logical mind began to seek answers as it attempted to understand what I was doing and how I did it. The quieter my mind got, the easier it became for me to tune into guidance. I learned that my body is an intelligence in and of itself; it was doing all of the latter in and of itself. I didn't teach it how to tune in. I didn't teach it how to become the person in front me. It's as if there was a line of code or a piece of memory in this biological suit that hosts me, and that code or memory was being activated.

I'm continuously humbled with how much I do not know and how much there is to learn. Not from books, but from simply being silent, spending time alone in nature, and listening to the wisdom of my body. What do I mean by wisdom of my body? Again, it will become clearer as you go through the book.

Going back to two years ago (2018)–after having this 'invisible cushion' lingering around me for a while–I started to acknowledge the repetitive number patterns I saw everywhere, whether it was on my phone, my laptop, license plates, oven clock, receipts, etc. Seriously, everywhere. The synchronicities and patterns were too obvious to ignore. Initially I had no clue what to do with the numbers. Later in time, I noticed that a certain series of numbers would show up together. I started to write them down. I then saw patterns and began to follow the breadcrumbs being left for me. I realized that was one method of communication with the unseen.

It didn't just come from the numbers. Guidance came in from all sorts of directions. A random book would be shoved into my hand. A random person would walk into my life and give me what I call the 'spiritual slap' or 'a nudge' to look in a different direction. Answers were everywhere: in my dreams and in every person I interacted with. It took all of it to make it all obvious for me.

Around that time, I concluded that I was living someone else's life, not mine. To be able to live my life, I needed to find out who I was, and what is it that I am, before I could lead a life that represented who I really am. Yes, that was when I let go and lived out of a suitcase. So now you have a slightly clearer picture of the events and the catalysts that led me on this path and journey.

It didn't take me too long, after starting my journey, to realize and then fully acknowledge that over time I'd become a prisoner to my body and mind's habit patterns–patterns that were not necessarily mine. I'd become a prisoner of their own habit pattern of life, simply succumbing to their wants and needs. Now that I've torn down the walls of this prison of which I'd not previously been aware, I'm eager to share with you the messages that have been coming through and to me. These broadcasts–available for everyone who's listening–have been teaching me and guiding me along this flight into freedom. Yes, I'm far from being special. It's just a matter of learning how to tune in.

I'm going to do my best to share what has come through in the most logical way I can. The honest truth is that most of what I've written down didn't come from my intellect. I've simply taken the many signals or broadcasts that I suddenly found myself tuned into and allowed them to come through in my writing. It started off for my own personal development. I realized that, a lot of the time, I learned from what I wrote down. Yes, I would re-read what I wrote and even, at times, it would take me a few reads to fully understand what's being said to me.

One thing's for sure, this experience and tough challenge have taught me a valuable lesson, and that's that there is no greater knowledge than the knowledge you have verified for yourself within the framework of your own body. No one can prove anything to anyone, because proof is based on what the other person chooses to believe. Period. I want you to examine the next sentence carefully. Everything that you live is what you believe. You can take a moment and sit with that sentence. Again, everything that you live is what you believe.

None of us are here to impose beliefs onto one another. It is your experience. At the end of the day, we are information-gathering species, and we're here to grow; we're here to learn. And as we do, we share what we've learned. Not for glory. Not for attention. We share because we know that there are other portions of ourselves, who are waiting on us to step up and share with them what we have learned objectively, without allowing our own belief systems to twist the knowledge/information that has come through.

For me, with my background of being hardened to ignore feelings and solely follow logical-based practicality, experiential knowledge of the truth was the only way to step into my liberation and learn yet another valuable lesson: to surrender to my soul; to surrender to my calling.

The

MINDCHEMIST

CHAPTER I

UNCERTAINTY

After many days of fasting in solitude in the Amazon jungle, I woke up to a hint of light stretching from the horizon and birds awakening into song. There was freshness in the air and an aliveness all around me. Inspired by how I felt in that moment, I decided to leave my simplistic hut and take a walk.

Some time passed and thoughts began to bubble up. I thought to myself how funny it was that I was actually there in the jungle. Not too long ago, I was attending a conference for work and, all of a sudden, I felt overwhelmed by all the people in attendance. A strong need to isolate myself followed that feeling. I walked outside the building, found a quiet spot, closed my eyes, took a deep breath in and disconnected from the loudness of my surroundings. As I slowed down, my eyes still closed, I found myself visualizing a jungle far away from civilization. I sat with that picture in my mind for some time, and, as some unsolicited tears ran down my face, I made an intention from the deepest portion of my heart to find such a jungle. I was confused. Why was I so emotional all of a sudden? I opened my eyes, wiped my face and went back to the other jungle–the one I was in. Fast forward a few weeks later, and there I was. Just like that.

Yet again reality was bending to my will. But how? Why? I had all these questions. What's really happening to me? How did I get here? I was living the life of my dreams, exactly the way I imagined myself to be living it, yet at my so-called peak I never felt so empty, so utterly empty. I cracked a laugh as I began to reflect back on how it all started, because it really is hilarious how oblivious I was to what was happening to me and how I was 'doing it' and transforming. It was all happening for me at a much subtler layer, a much subtler reality than what we usually think of as our reality.

I began to trace the last series of events that got me to where I was that day in the jungle. It started when I moved to Northern California (San Francisco Bay Area) for a job, and I found myself playing soccer again. I pulled a muscle while I was playing one day, and a friend recommended yoga as a way to stretch my leg and help me recover faster. I went to one class and I was hooked. In a matter of weeks, I found myself dropping to previously unknown levels of this reality.

Living and working in the heart of Silicon Valley, in a stressful environment, suddenly became much easier. My control over the soccer ball during games improved, and those 'high-stakes' meetings where 'the deal' was on the line also became a cinch. I started to see them for what they actually were. Whenever I needed to make an important decision, I waited until after my yoga class before deciding.

Holy moly, stretching my legs, ha! I initially thought, and then, but wait a minute ... what's up with this yoga thing? I'm curious now.

No longer was I interested in high tech (what I did for a living) as much as I was interested in learning more about this body of mine, this mind of mine ... Who am I? What is I? Hmm. Why do I do the things I do? Why do I choose to work long hours, and why do I choose to work on weekends when I don't have to? Hmm. Why does recognition from others no longer tickle my fancy? Why isn't money fulfilling me? Why is this life no longer cranking up? Why? Why? Why? But I swear I wanted all of this, and I worked hard to get to where I am!

Then looking back that day in the jungle, I realized it was around the time when I had all those questions that I found myself at a boat party in San Francisco that I hadn't wanted to go to but went to because my gut told me to be there. There I ran into a beautiful soul, and as we talked, she brought up Vipassana (one of India's most ancient meditation techniques, rediscovered by Gautama Buddha more than 2500 years ago). She didn't say much about it, she just said to me, "It changed my life, and if you're meant to do it, then you'll know."

A couple of weeks after that boat party, I woke up in the middle of the night and registered for a Vipassana course. I only remembered that I'd registered for it the next morning when I received a confirmation email. Strangely, the course I'd signed up for was in Quebec, yet I lived in California, but with all that was going on with me at the time, nothing seemed to surprise me anymore.

As I let go of my identity, my job, the money and all that built up my ego at the time, I initially felt that I lost my power, and my mind was full of fear and doubt. No logical sense backed up my actions, but it felt like the right thing to do, so I just went with it anyway. A few days into my Vipassana course, I began to remember ... Vipassana was no stranger to me. The people in that room were not strangers. Confused, I wondered why Vipassana was so familiar. Again I asked myself: What's happening to me? Why all of this? Who can I talk to? What's all this change about? Am I losing my mind?

Though my mind had gone back to that time, my body was still wandering through the Amazon. I stopped and looked around, interrupting my train of thoughts. Why am I here in the jungle? How did I even get here?

I took off my Crocs, allowing my feet to touch the Earth, took a deep breath in and appreciated some of the cleanest air I've ever

3

inhaled. As I exhaled, I felt and heard my heart beating fast while my mind was on a mission of its own, trying to trace and make sense of the series of events that had brought me to the jungle. I looked to my right, saw a suitable rock and sat down to give my legs a break.

Then out of nowhere, a pleasant, calm and centered inner voice said, "Hey. You. Yes, you. Take a chill pill. I know patience isn't your strong suit, so I'm going to skip the pleasantries and cut to the chase. Look, I know you have a lot of questions, and I get it, but I do want you to do me a favor before we even get started, and that is, not to try to over analyze everything we talk about today, but rather allow it all to filter through you. It will all make more sense later on when you discover your emotional body. You're well in the process. Stay with me, right here, right now, in this moment and allow yourself to listen intently and openly to what I have to share with you. You're extremely intellectual and, as such, your knee-jerk reaction will be to try to reason with everything that comes out of my mouth, but what I'm asking you to do is to pause and listen."

I was taken off guard by the clarity and intrusiveness of the voice that had filled my head. "What? Who's this?" I said to myself. "What's going on?" And how did this voice know me so well?

"I have so much I want to share with you," the voice continued. "You're gifted in ways that you, in your current perception, can't imagine just yet. They're asking me to slow down and be mindful of your state right now."

Confused, I reacted, asking "What? Wait ... Who's asking you to ask me to slow down?"

"Listen. I understand the confusion. Here's the deal ... I'm going to do most of the talking for the next little while, because I don't want you to be swayed by what you want to hear from me. I'd rather focus on what they wish you to know first. Yes, you want to know who they are right now, but at the deepest level of the mind you already know, and intellectually you'll know who they are later on today. They're very happy and excited for you. They have so much to share with you. That's why I want you to practice listening for now, so you can finally hear the answers to the gazillion questions that you've been asking."

"That's exactly what I am looking for!" I replied.

"Again, I get it," the voice went on, "and I understand that you've been under a lot of pressure. I can feel your anxiety, and I'm really trying to feel sorry for you, but for some reason, I just don't have it in me. Oh, I know why; it's because I know something you don't know ... I know something you don't know ... yes, I'm teasing you, and no, not to get on your nerves but to lighten you up a little; you're too serious about it all."

"That's easy for you to say." I replied.

"The information I have to share with you has the potential to completely shift your entire future moving forward. I'm being nudged to address the concept of future right off the bat. I hate to break it to you, but I can't predict the future for you or tell you exactly what's coming up ahead. That's why it's important for you to understand how the future truly works, so you can begin to understand that much of what you want, and much of the answers you seek, can and will be found inside you. It's never been about you needing to seek something outside of yourself to obtain what you want or to fulfill your needs. I lost you right there, but it'll all make sense very soon.

"What's going on with you right now is that a shift of perception is coming your way. You've been seeking this, and now it's here. You've known it was coming. Now it's arrived, it's not very gentle, so to speak, and it's giving birth to some overwhelming feelings that you're trying to make sense of, and that's why I'm here. That's why you're in the jungle right now. That's why you want to spend some time alone. I'm going to do my best to be very logical with you because that's how your brain prefers to work, for now."

I fidgeted. The rock suddenly felt hard beneath me and the trees too close and too thick.

"I can feel that you're getting uncomfortable because you don't know where you are exactly or where you're headed today on this walk. Heck, you don't even know to whom you're talking. To top it all off, you don't know who they are, but again, amongst all of these unknowns, do me a favor and loosen up today, and let those feelings pass through you. Don't try to resist and control them, rather, just observe them, acknowledge them and allow them to pass without reacting to them. And really listen without letting your past thoughts, experiences and beliefs take over and pull you away from this moment, because where your thoughts go, your energy follows.

"Now—since we're keeping it real—you're a tough nut to crack. Your attention is so laser focused on getting certain information in a certain way that you tend not to allow yourself to see and access the rest of the information that's coming in through different ways, so you can't see the picture in its totality. Especially right now, when you're on this epic journey of exploration, it's not the time to narrow the field; it's time to widen it. Don't look for the narrowing; look for the widening, so more can come through, and more can inspire you, and then you can move on to the next stages.

"The journey is exploratory, the journey is exciting, the journey needs to be loose. I know you want to have some ends tied up, but I see looseness. I see freedom. You're wanting freedom above all. You want to feel free. You don't want to feel as though you're answerable and have to do this and have to do that and have to do that other thing, do you?"

I nodded. He was right.

"And yet," the voice continued, "in your thinking you're wanting the narrowing, and I'm encouraging you to open the thinking and to say freedom is my number one priority. Because it really is. The freer you can feel, the easier your life will get, and you'll be able to pay attention to all the signals that you're getting but not noticing.

"In your meditation yesterday, you told me that it's getting harder for you to differentiate between what's real and what's not. Okay, let's take a step back. I feel that I'm playing with your energy, and that's not my intention. It feels this way because what's happening right now is that there are two personalities trying to mix here. I am needing to be very calm, yet you are somewhat tense because there's a lot of pressure on you. Although you don't know it yet, you've voluntarily put all this pressure on your own shoulders. Yes, I said voluntarily, and if you haven't noticed, today we're going to get comfortable talking about uncomfortable stuff. Today is about us–what you perceive to be you and what you perceive to be I having a slightly unusual yet epic dance.

"I like the smile you have on your face right now. I'm being asked to say this firmly to you–and it's going to keep that smile going–you are always protected every step of the way. Nothing bad will happen to you, not now or moving forward in your life. Now, does that mean that you can go ahead and chuck yourself under a bus or a train and nothing will happen to you, although you're intentionally being reckless? No, but it means that when you pay attention to your intuition as well as your logic, there is no such thing as making the wrong choice when it comes to your life.

"Don't you find it interesting that rather than being fully immersed and curious about where you are right now, surrounded by all this natural beauty, you choose to be anxious, because you don't know where you are exactly, when you can choose to soak in all this beauty that surrounds you and have faith that you'll find your way? Yes, I know you don't do it intentionally. I bring this up simply to nudge you to notice and observe certain patterns in your behavior.

"See ... it's this same pattern of behavior that keeps repeating itself. Every time you find yourself in a situation where you can't really predict or know what's going to happen next, that situation triggers a feeling of you not being in control based on your current perception of life. This feeling is fueling this reactive behavioral pattern of anxiety, which is triggered by your own need for safety and security. Now tell me; where do safety and security come from in a situation like this?

When it might seem that you're lost and can't see what's coming up ahead in the future? I can tell you one thing for sure, you can't, and won't, find them from a place of logic alone–from a place of wanting to grind up, measure and then count in order to try to establish if it's going to measure and count the same tomorrow. In a situation like this, you'll want to use more than just your logic to make your way through. But most importantly, I want you to ask yourself: what is it that you're seeking safety and security from? What is it that you want to control exactly? Why do you want to be in control?"

CHAPTER 2

CONTROL

"Control?" I replied, giving voice to my introspection. "That makes a lot of sense. I'm not necessarily aware that I'm wanting control all the time. Nor am I aware that I'm seeking safety and security. Although, now that I think about it, there is truth to what you're saying, but still it's not clear why I've developed this habit of seeking safety and security. And I'm not sure what it is I'm wanting to control." I spoke as if the voice sat next to me.

The voice replied immediately, "Yes, it all seems jumbled up at the moment, but I know what's going to clear the fog for you. Remember your last trip to Barcelona when you and Morgan went horseback riding and joined that group of seven people? The first thing that Juan, the owner of the ranch, asked the group was, 'How many of you have ridden a horse before?' You and a couple of other people raised your hands. He then pointed to three horses; the ones on the far left-hand side and, with a smile on his face, said, 'Okay, then; the three of you will be riding these three horses. Don't worry, there's nothing wrong with those horses; they just need a little more handling.'

I remembered the time. Juan had then said, "Before we take the horses for a ride today, I first want to share with you a few brief lessons from my humble lifetime experience working with horses. This will allow you to have a good understanding of how they think so that you can truly enjoy your experience today. Horses are high-spirited animals, full of energy. They like to be free and play outside." He pointed to all nine horses and with a slight change in tone added, "These horses–heck there's no right way of saying this–they've lost connection to their souls. Now they stay here all day. I use them to take tourists like yourself on rides around the area, and then I bring them right back here. That's their life now.

"When you get on your assigned horse today and get on the path, the first thing the horse is going to do is to test you by trying to steer you off the path and eat from the shrubs and grass along the sides of the path. But, trust me, the horses aren't hungry. I feed them well. The horse does that because he's trying to figure out whether or not you know what you're doing.

"When the horse tries to steer you off track, I want you to firmly pull on the strap and bring the horse back on the path that it's supposed to be on, even if you feel that it might be uncomfortable for the horse. Please pull firmly. Simple, but not easy."

I remembered us all nodding sagely.

"That's right." The voice took over the story. "And then comes the really interesting bit, when the ranch owner said, 'Establishing this trust with the horse is of paramount importance for both of your sakes. See, if the horse thinks that you–the rider–don't know what you're doing, then the horse will decide to take over. He'll think, 'This dude has no clue what he's doing; there's no way I'm going to let him take control and lead the way. I need to, I have to, I must take care of both of us.'

"'On the other hand, if the horse feels that you know what you're doing, then you're well in the process of establishing that

10

much-needed trust between you, and you're successfully taming your horse. That's when the horse begins to slowly let go of control, gently release resistance and develop faith and trust that it's being guided and taken care off by you, the rider. There's nothing more the horse wants than to surrender all the worry, all the burdens and all the headaches that come with the responsibility behind all the decision making that needs to be done when one's leading the way. The horse would love to take all of it, put it in a box, wrap it in a nice bow and hand it over to you so that it can finally just be, and taste the freedom that comes with just being in the moment, being in the present that you've gifted it. Then it begins to enjoy its ride fully and notice and soak-in all the beauty that surrounds it.'

"Do you see where I'm heading with this story?" the voice asked me. "This jungle ... you ... you're not so different, dear one. The horse you were taking for a ride is your mind, and the person riding the horse is you, the dude inside. (Dude is unisex. Just in case your mind wandered elsewhere already). Yes, my dear, now you're beginning to understand what I meant when I said, what you perceive to be you and what you perceive to be I earlier on.

"I know it's confusing. I'm intentionally confusing you because I want you to get out of the grogginess and staleness of the mundane, out of this habit of wanting to be spoon-fed information and instead allow the creative juices to flow. Trust your instinct on who I is and who you is, and it will all be addressed on this walk today."

At his mention of walking, I heaved myself off the rock and carried on down the path. Maybe I didn't know where I was, but I was on a path, even if I didn't know where it led. I could always turn around and go back.

"You've never spent a moment by yourself," the voice continued. "The dude inside has always been with you. He's been trying to get your attention your entire life. And he knows your path, just like you knew that you were going to take that horse for a half an hour ride on that path just outside the ranch, and that you were coming back to drop off the horse at the ranch before you continued on your journey elsewhere. The dude inside also knows what you came here to do in the first place, and why. You guys were simply in a different type of ranch before you came here."

I'm glad that at least part of me knows what's going on, I thought sarcastically.

The voice ignored me and barreled on, "The feelings of discomfort the horse felt when it resisted your guidance as you pulled on the strap, trying to bring the horse back onto the path, are analogous to the discomfort and dis-ease you've felt because, similar to the horse, you've been resisting the guidance of the dude inside, the rider, as he tries to bring you back on track to fulfilling your true desires, even though you might not be aware of them just yet. You resist him because you don't trust him and are too afraid to surrender and let go of the steering wheel."

I had to admit this was making a lot of sense.

"Although you, quite literally, don't know where you're going and can't see what tomorrow holds, still you choose to be in control, and you choose to ignore the subtle signals, subtle emotions that have been guiding you all along. Just like what the horse was doing to you in the beginning ... up until you gained its trust.

"Being on the path that fulfills you has nothing to do with making a lot of money or material success. Well, I don't need to tell you this. You've experienced it. And just like the rider of the horse, there's nothing more your soul wants than to help your mind let go of the illusion of fear that has been programmed into you. There's nothing more your soul wants from your mind than for it to trust and truly have faith in the dude inside, and for your mind to take the backseat and offload the exhaustion that comes with all the decision making onto your soul, to the dude inside. It's a process, and you're well in it."

12

Pleased to hear that, I nodded. The path levelled off a little and I increased my pace accordingly.

The voice carried on with its monologue. "Soon your mind will reach a point where it'll trust that the dude inside knows what he's doing and that he can take care of it and of this vehicle, then, slowly, it will let go and surrender. That's all there is to it. It's a matter of gaining its trust. Like I said earlier: it's a dance. The whole process is a slightly awkward yet epic dance.

"You see now? Because you're constantly running, serving your mind's agenda day after day, you don't stop and take time to breathe and observe your behavior."

I stopped, took a deep breath and concentrated on his words. They hit me somewhere deep inside.

"What you do, what you say, how you do it, how you say it, why do you even do any of it? And how much of your behavior is automatic and reactive in its nature? And how much of it do you really have control of? As such you continuously give your mind the upper hand that it always had on the dude inside, and it decides not to let the dude inside give you the answers that you so eagerly seek.

"Hence, you end up thinking, and eventually believing, that you don't have the answers and that you don't know what you want. And, no, the mind doesn't do that intentionally to hurt you, but simply because it doesn't know any better. It reverts back to its operating system, back to its belief system, and creates based on what it believes. This is what I meant earlier when I said that you already have all the answers you're seeking within—although at a logical level, you might still 'believe' otherwise. Remember that everything you live is what you believe.

"I'll be repeating this again and again until it fully registers. Your soul, just like the rider, is saying, 'Dude, slow down and hear me out; I got you. I know what's up. Don't resist me and make this harder on both of us. Just allow me to guide you. From where I stand, I can

13

see the whole picture. I see the owner of the ranch, the ranch itself, the path and the plan for the journey. I know the end goal. Deep down you don't want to be in control, dear one. You want to simply be. You want to enjoy the ride. You want to soak in all this beauty that surrounds you. You want to be free. You want to give away to me all your thinking, aka all your worries and anxieties about not knowing what's coming up ahead and whether or not you're making the right choices in life. That's what your soul wants you to know. That's what I want you to know. You are safe and guided."

CHAPTER 3

OUT OF BALANCE

I continued my walk, feeling as if a weight had been lifted off my shoulders. I felt warmth, protection and clarity. At the same time, my mind attempted to find a crack in what the voice just said, so it could challenge it. I laughed as I observed my mind's knee-jerk reaction. *Why,* I asked it, *are you wanting to find a way to prove that what the voice said is not true?*

And it was very clear to me that my mind wasn't trying to challenge or prove that the voice was somehow wrong or that there was a crack in what the voice said; it had simply been accustomed to allow information to come in specific and certain ways that are generally more tangible and fact oriented. Now it's receiving truth that it's wanting to allow to come in, but it doesn't know how to allow it to do that. But it knows it's true from the wisdom of the body, from how the body felt.

That's when I started to train the mind to use the wisdom of the body as another input, another source of information that it can use in its decision-making process. Slowly but surely, I became more and more compassionate to my mind and more and more understanding of what simply is, without judgement. I have my Vipassana practice to thank for this. I'll be diving deep into my Vipassana experience in later chapters.

The voice returned, saying, "See the two small waterfalls up ahead? Let's take a dip in the water."

I smiled. The water looked so clear and fresh and inviting. I stripped off my T-shirt and eased myself into the water. The first few steps were dangerously slippery; a lot of algae covered the shallow end of the water where I entered. It was so slippery that I decided to use all my limbs. I lay on my belly and made my way to the waterfalls. The water got deeper the closer I got to the falls. I found a good comfortable rock to sit on right under one of the falls. It was perfect. Relaxed in my body, I allowed the water to massage my neck.

The voice continued, "Ever since you were a kid, you've been curious about life and how things worked in this culture medium that you found yourself in. Because of your curiosity and your discipline, combined with the handful of times where you trusted yourself fully and let yourself be guided 'unknowingly'—aka listened to your intuition without questioning yourself, mind intervening,—you've accomplished what's known to you in your current perceived world as success. As such you've proved to yourself that you can have as much of this so-called 'success' as you want. And now all of a sudden, you're perplexed and confused as to why you've never felt so utterly empty inside, although from the outside you're living the life that you've always wanted to live—exactly the way you pictured it in your mind when you were younger. Which brings us to your sudden need to seek out the truth. The truth in its totality for once. The universal truth.

"All right. How do I put this gently? Ahh, nevermind. You're a big boy. You can take it. A lot of your thought process is mitigated by the fact that your belief system is deeply rooted in fear. The worst part is that, because it's so subtle, this belief system of yours makes you decide not to allow yourself to think or even dare question things that you've been taught, things that you've been told and have accepted to be the so-called 'norm' in your culture medium and beyond. And no, you're not aware that this is the case, and no, you don't do this to yourself knowingly or intentionally. Again, keeping it one hundo here–you're not the only one. Remember don't take anything personal. I love you, but this is much bigger than you.

In this particular moment right now, I feel very strongly that whatever you're dealing with at a subconscious level has a lot to do with attachments to your past. I'm being drawn to a parent figure. What this tells me is that whatever is being triggered at this point in your life–which is a period of restructuring, to say the least–is connected somehow to your father. Your father did exactly what he was supposed to do. He played his role to the T.

He took care of you, pampered you and protected you–a little too much if you ask me. He loves you from the bottom of his heart. But this is about you understanding the character and the role he had to play in your life, the subconscious way you're connected and why you make the choices and decisions that you make in your day to day life. You'll find that a lot of the choices you make are based purely on safety and security first. Yes, that's where it comes from."

I interrupted the voice and asked him, "What's wrong with making choices and decisions that are purely based on safety and security first? I don't see anything wrong with that. In fact, it makes a lot of sense to me."

The voice replied, "Absolutely nothing. There is nothing wrong with that. I never said it was wrong. Here's the thing: in life when you favor one particular thing, one particular point of view, desire, feeling, object over anything and everything else, you'll find yourself in a place where you'll be looking for something more. Because that one thing will not be enough for you and will not be able to fully satisfy you. Again, I don't need to tell you this. You've experienced this yourself. All I'm doing right now is pointing it out for you. This is the root cause behind why you are where you are right now, and that is out of balance.

"You're learning not to get sucked into one thing; you're learning not to take sides, not to be fixed to one way of thinking, not to be influenced to seeing life through one set of glasses. Especially not through someone else's set of glasses that they made for you. Rather to be in harmony with it all, starting with yourself. You can dumb it down to when that one hit song comes out on the radio, and you like it so much that you put that song on repeat, because you just love the beat, but then suddenly one day you're just fed up with listening to that same song. Although it's the same song that used to make you want to dance, now, you choose not to listen to it anymore. Balance.

"See ... you need, and you want, variety in your life. In fact, you thrive in such an environment. Because, truly, you're here for the experience of being in human form. That's it. It's that simple. Nothing more, nothing less. I'll repeat it again. You are here to experience what it's like to be in human form. Yes, you heard me loud and clear; deep down you seek experience. That's what this whole thing is about. You coming to Earth was never about material abundance. Although you can have as much of it as you want along this journey, but it's not the be-all and end-all.

"Ultimately, you want to allow yourself to experience life and all the variety it has to offer. When you allow yourself to fully experience it, and be present with what you're experiencing, you'll learn, grow and expand beyond what you can currently conceive of. The key here is to be present with what you are experiencing.

"The potent power of being present with what you're experiencing allows you to express a unique energetic life force that can only be translated through you and shared with the world through the full expression of who you really are. In plain English, you came here to fully express yourself. Ask yourself: are you living life fully? Do you allow yourself to express your authentic truth? Do you even allow yourself to be completely you when you're out there in the world?

"You don't have to answer me or feel that you have to give me an answer right now. Simply allow the answers to arise when they arise. When I question you, I'm not necessarily seeking specific answers, my dear. I'm simply activating your curiosity."

I suddenly came back to my sensations and felt the water from the waterfall wash over me again. At that moment, I did feel completely 'me.'

"So you see," the voice continued, "this energy of you needs and wants variety, yet you, in your current conditioned thinking, have been trained to narrow your vision, suppress your creativity and focus on what you've been so gently influenced to focus on—irrelevant to what you really want for yourself. You're constantly reacting to your surroundings and focusing on what you're going through rather than what and who you're becoming. Ultimately, being steered away from finding out who you are, and, as such, steered away from expressing yourself fully. That's why I'm reminding you to always come back to your center and cultivate balance in your day to day, so you can see the distortion, act from a place of clarity and have a sense of who you are. How are you supposed to express yourself if you don't know who you are? Once again, no, you don't do this to yourself intentionally, and did I mention that it's much bigger than you?"

Out of curiosity I asked the voice, "When did all of this start? How did I fall out of balance?" My mind activated and shifted from being curious to being angry. I went from calm to seeking proof, but I didn't have proof. I didn't want to accept that I didn't know who I was. I didn't want to accept that I've been conditioned to narrow my vision. So I asked, "How do I know if I'm aligned with my authentic truth and living a life of my own? How do I know if I'm simply reacting to my surroundings or acting from a place of knowing? How do I know if I'm being influenced and off balanced? Is there some sort of guidance system that can guide me and help me discern what's right for me and what's not?"

CHAPTER 4

FEELING CENTER

I could hear a smile in the voice's tone as he said, "I have you exactly where I want you ... this is the type of questioning I want you to cultivate more of in your life. You can go so far by allowing yourself to question what you hear, what you see and what you're being told. From your own experience, you can see how life is understood backwards as you live it forwards. Meaning, there's a reason why you went through what you went through.

"You've gained invaluable experiential knowledge of how it feels to have those experiences. The latter sentence is extremely powerful. In it you'll find the answers to the questions that you just asked me. My intent is never to give you the answers. My intent is to guide you to find your own answers. You have been accustomed to seeking answers from outside of you and fall into complacency. I seek to activate you. I seek to show you how powerful you are. And yes, I seek to prove to you from your own experiences–since you love this word 'proof'–that you already have the answers you're seeking. You're simply not practiced enough to find them yourself just yet.

"On this journey you'll reach many breakthroughs and self-realizations. There'll be times—and we'll be covering more of this later today—but there'll be times when you'll uncover certain truths and discover certain portions or aspects of yourself that you won't necessarily want to accept. Because you don't yet understand how they're your greatest teachers, and how much you can learn by shedding light onto those aspects of you.

"Yes, it won't be comfortable sometimes, but remember what we talked about. Come back to your center. Don't allow those emotions and feelings to pull you away from your center. The anger that just arose from you when you were asking me those questions didn't come by itself. Anger doesn't just pass by for a visit and say, 'Hi.' You create the anger. Deep down you don't want to create anger or any sort of resentfulness. You want to stay curious and objectively observe your experience. We'll dive deeper into the latter concepts later. For now, remember that you want to open new channels of information, so that more can come to you in whatever way it wants to come. Observe how this information makes you feel, but don't allow it to throw you off. I'll remind you of this because it's much easier said than done."

I pulled my head out from under the waterfall, and a fresh breeze of air came in and cooled the heat of the sun off my face. My mind twirled from all the information, but despite all the words, my questions remained unanswered.

"Now to answer your questions," the voice, clearly party to my thoughts, said, "I want you to take a snapshot of your recent past. You went to university to study one thing, although you were thirsty for knowledge of all things. Topics existed that you didn't know about, so you couldn't know if you might be interested in them, all simply because they weren't part of the so-called 'Educational System.' Why? Well, that's a tangent for another day.

"Now, remember that time, towards the end of the first year of your undergraduate degree, when you experienced all sorts of overwhelming feelings? What did you do with those feelings? Did you take time to understand what they were telling you? Or did you ignore them and go straight back into doing the same thing that gave birth to those feelings in the first place? Of course, you didn't listen to your feelings. A tough man ignores their feelings. Even better, he resists them, suppresses them and 'powers through them,' right?

"The real question here, is why do you continue to do things that you don't want to do? And why do you feel that you have to do them or else? Then ask yourself, when did you become so hardened and quite rigid in your beliefs and in your understandings? When did you become afraid of your own emotions and your own feelings?"

Agitated by his words, I responded, "Who told you I'm afraid? I'm not afraid. I have no fear." I clambered out of the water and slumped petulantly against a rock.

The voice continued, "We tend to fear what we don't understand. Fear isn't a bad thing. We'll address this concept of judging something as good and bad later. But I want you to understand that fear, once understood, can be an ally.

"No one taught you how to discern your feelings. When they come at you, you have no clue what to do. You tell yourself you're not afraid, and you suppress them and you move on. That's where you trick yourself. The underlying truth, dear one, is that you are afraid to feel, and that's why you run away, ignore and supress your feelings. That's simply fear of what you don't understand. That's all there is to it. Again, don't take this personal. Because it's not. Don't be thrown off your center.

"Moving forward, I'm telling you to trust your feelings and understand what they're telling you, and go through them, no matter what they are. No matter how uncomfortable they are, your feelings are your best teachers and guides. It's not that you don't know how to

23

feel. It's the same for you as it is for the horse when you're guiding it by pulling firmly on the reins to bring it back on its path; that pulling might cause what you consider discomfort or pain. But just like the horse, you're afraid of your feelings–guides–because you don't trust them, and you don't know what to do with them when you have them. They bring up a sense of powerlessness within you, so you end up associating that feeling with weakness. That's why you got agitated earlier and told me with an angry tone that you are not afraid. You're beginning to understand that the root cause of suffering operates at a much deeper level of the mind and not simply at the intellectual level of the mind.

"Now tell me, according to whom are feelings considered a weakness? Where did this belief come from? This is a perfect time for you to grow a pair and stop tiptoeing around your emotions. It's time to see things as they really are, and not as how you would like them to be or think they should be. That's where you limit your experience. That's one source of where your anger comes from–judgement. And because you judge yourself against how you think you should be, you automatically judge others, even if you're not aware of it at the surface level of the mind. But now our focus is on you.

"When you begin to see things as they are for what they are, that's when you begin to move past judgment and allow yourself to feel all the ways that you feel no matter how uncomfortable some feelings might seem to you. That's when you'll get to some powerful breakthroughs, because now you have acknowledged the feeling, and you're listening to what it's trying to tell you. You're listening to what it's trying to teach you, and you're no longer dodging the issue so you can think that you're a tough dude, or that you're in control. You're starting to understand now what I meant earlier when I told you, 'Don't try to resist and control the feelings, rather just observe them, acknowledge them and allow them to pass without reacting to them.' I can feel that's clearing up for you. It's only going to get clearer from here.

"Going back to that time when you experienced all sorts of overwhelming feelings. With the perception that you had back then, you considered it 'normal' that you were in pain. You considered it normal that pain is a part of life, and the right thing to do at the time was not to give up and go through pain. You powered through what might have been a hard time in your life when that hard time didn't need to exist at all. It could've been much easier had you known that your feelings speak your ultimate truth—like the rider pulling on the horse—and that the discomfort you felt was simply a byproduct of your own resistance to your own inner guidance system. Yep, just like the horse.

"You accepted things for what they were at the time without questioning them. It seemed like the right thing to do, since everyone with whom you shared your thoughts and feelings at the time told you it was just a phase you were going through and that you should keep yourself busy and it would soon all be over. That was when you picked up a skill that humanity has come to master, the art of suppression of feelings.

"Next time you find yourself in a situation of pain, don't run away and suppress that feeling but rather face it and ask yourself, 'Why am I in pain? What is this feeling trying to tell me? Is it possible to live a life without pain? Where does my belief that pain is a part of life come from? When and where was I exposed to this conditioning?'

"Now I want you to hear this firmly: conditioning is a part of this play of life; you cannot avoid it, nor would you want to avoid it. It's not the detriment here; ignorance—that is to 'ignore what is'—is the only detriment.

"When you first gain awareness of your conditioning, your initial reaction might be to rebel or get angry at those who participated in that conditioning, but the truth is you don't want to do that. What you really want to do is understand your conditioning

25

and how it impacts your mental, emotional and physical being as you begin to lead a life as yourself–it's time you tamed the wild horse and tapped into you. Tap into the dude inside, and as you slowly allow him to tame the wild horse of the mind, you'll be able to finally use all of the mind's enormous power to serve yourself, and as you serve yourself, you serve others. It's very important that you understand that you do your greatest work with yourself. Serving others is simply a byproduct. This too will become clearer.

"Like I said, conditioning is a portion of this game of life, and before you came here, you knew you were going to be conditioned and that there'll be a time when you'll get yourself out of it. Yes, that's why one of the first things I told you today was that you already knew that a change of perception was coming. Because it's through that process where the real learning and the real growth happens for the soul.

"You selected your culture medium and your parents, because it was in that nest that you could do your greatest growth. You might not be able to see it just yet, but you were born in the most ideal situation. Your parents are your guardians, and they structure your belief system, and they structure your thoughts. Now, for your own growth and development, is the time to examine your basic beliefs and begin to understand where they come from and the role that your parents had to play.

"As you go through those beliefs objectively, you might find that some of them no longer fit who you're becoming, and if that's the case, then it's time to let them go. Thank them for their service, and then bid them farewell. It's not that different from cleaning your closet and going through your clothes and picking out the pieces that no longer fit you. This is what you want to do with your thoughts as well. Thoughts that no longer fit and enhance your experience, simply discard them.

"Get rid of all of your old behavioral patterns and teachings

that no longer serve you, and then mentally forgive those who participated in giving you those beliefs. Many factors and influences played
a role, but your parents played a major role in shaping your belief system. Love them and forgive them for what they didn't know to teach
you, and forgive yourself for judging them for what you think they
didn't do for you. They have done so much for you that if you spent
your entire lifetime repaying them, it wouldn't be enough. I mean
they literally wiped your ass.

Now, as you discard thoughts that no longer serve you, you'll
immediately feel lighter and begin to move forward in your life.
Like I said before, you will re-pattern and affect many others from
your own personal growth. I hope you can now clearly see that you're
the lump of clay you're designing and working with. Keep reminding
yourself again and again that you're working with yourself. Your work
is work within your thoughts. As you work with your thoughts, you
begin to change the world you occupy. Take a moment to allow this
to soak in."

I eased myself over to the edge of the rock on which I sat,
put my feet in the water and swished them about as I thought of my
parents and myself in this new light. Something released deep inside
me. I took a deep breath and exhaled slowly.

"Notice right now your energy," the voice continued. "It's
completely shifted. Do you feel that? What happened? You're much
more relaxed, less combative and more in a receptive state all of a
sudden. Ask yourself what was it that I said that made you go silent?
Am I telling you things that you already know? Or thoughts that
have bubbled up before, but you decided to ignore them because they
were too subtle for you to take them seriously? Everything I brought
up today and will bring up has a purpose. That sounded pretentious,
but, again, I'm keeping it real. It's the truth. Sometimes I don't even
know the purpose behind what I say, and even I have to go and ask
them for guidance.

27

"The reason why I was asked to pay attention to this subtle shift of energy in you is so you can finally acknowledge the fact that you already know deep inside many of the things that you're seeking. What you're looking for is a confirmation or affirmation that you're right.

"There's a difference between the latter and not knowing all together. I'm having this conversation with you merely to provide your eager logical mind with the confirmation that yes, Mr. Mind, you are right, and yes, you want to start listening intently to your intuition rather than hearing and immediately ignoring these subtle feelings that your intuition uses to talk to you.

"In other words, your mind has been doing what it's been trained to do all these years, which is to allow your logic to take over what it is that's you, and you end up looking for affirmations and confirmations from sources outside of you. Why? Because you can see, hear, feel, taste and sense them with your senses, which soothes your mind because it's deemed logical and tangible."

A sense of calmness came over me. Relaxed in my body, I became more conscious of the warmth of the water. In that moment of relaxation, I looked to my right and witnessed a frog (which turned out to be a tree frog) quite literally skydive from one tree to a leaf on another tree. I smiled, and after a few moments of observing the frog, I said to the voice, "I understand what you're saying now. I am wanting to see more clearly. However, I do have a question for you. You told me that I'm here for the experience. The word experience, to me, sounds and feels free. It sounds exciting. There's a sense of adventure to it. But why, in this experience I'm having, aren't I feeling that I'm free?"

CHAPTER 5

FREEDOM

The voice replied to my question about not feeling free with, "When I first tuned into your frequency, I asked 'what does he really want and is looking for but isn't aware of?' The answer was very simple and very clear. The word freedom came to me. You're at the point in your evolution in this human body where, in order for you to be truly fulfilled, you want to feel free. This was one of the first things I shared with you this morning. Freedom means different things to different people. There's the generic meaning of freedom, but what does freedom mean to you? What does it mean to you?"

I paused and then said, "Is this a trick question? What do you mean, what does freedom mean to me? It means I want to be free. I want to do whatever my heart desires."

"Good," the voice replied. "You already know what you want. You want to be free. You want to be able to do what you want to do, however you want to do it, whenever you want to do it, whereever you want to do it and you want to do it your way. And by the way, they are telling me that you tend to make things way and I mean waaayy more complicated than what they really are. Why? Because

29

you tend to question yourself a lot."

"That's true." I nodded, then asked, "Why do I do that?"

"You already know the answer," the voice replied softly. "You do that because your perception is rooted in doubt. Doubt is rooted in the belief that you can't. But if you look back in time, you'll notice that you've proved to yourself many times within this particular lifetime that you can, even when you were put in situations that seemed impossible at the time."

As soon as the voice shared that, I felt synapses fire in my brain. I had this sudden urge to speak and express myself. Although I'd initially experienced a lot of resistance to what the voice had shared with me, deep down something inside of me wanted me to listen, and I'm glad I did. In that moment, I thought to myself, I think I know what this guy is talking about. When he said that I'd proved to myself that I could, even in situations that seemed impossible, he was talking about an experience I'd had at university. I'd completely forgotten about it. But I recalled it then.

As I'd approached my last year of university, I reached a point where I was fed up with the repetitive routine, so I decided to wrap it up, and hence I took the maximum amount of credits allowed. I remember having the need to talk to the chair of my department for approval. But the final exams period was approaching, and I was dealing with six advanced-level engineering courses.

The school I went to didn't give a grace period for studying before finals. For example, if the last day of school was Monday, then finals started Tuesday. The final exams schedule came out, and it looked like this: Monday, I had to hand in my project; Tuesday, I had two exams; Wednesday was off; Thursday, I had two exams, and Friday I had one last exam early in the morning. In order to hand in the project for Monday, I pulled yet another all-nighter—lack of sleep was a norm for me at the time—and after handing in the project, I had to study for my exams the following day despite my exhaustion. I asked myself, which one should I study for first? The 9 am one? Or the 2 pm one? Hmm. When I began to think that way, anxiety rose, and then I remembered how exhausted I was and that I had many more exams coming up back to back–some on subjects where I'd not attended class for a long time. To top it all off, the I must get an A mentality kicked in, and that's the cherry on top of this pile of anxiety.

Ahh! I'm overwhelmed, I told myself. So I took deep breaths and reminded myself to focus on one thing at a time. I studied for my 2 pm exam first, and later in the evening, I began to study for my 9 am one. When I suddenly discovered it was five in the morning already, I went to bed to rest before heading out to my exams. Around that time, I'd begun to feel a lag between my body and mind as the exhaustion of the past weeks piled up. It's a weird feeling. I'd tell my legs to walk, but their responsiveness was slow. First time I'd ever experience latency between my body and mind.

Nevertheless, I was able to make it to both of my exams, and it turned out well. I remember coming back at night with a mind so active that I couldn't sleep, yet my body was so tired it couldn't move. I made it through the night and had a whole day on Wednesday to study for my two exams the following day. The first was at 2 pm and the second at 6 pm. But I was in no way ready for either of them.

I cycled through anxiety and thinking about how exhausted I was and how I couldn't think straight, but I powered through as usual and went to bed the following day at 7 am. A few hours later at 10 am, I woke to review my notes, after which I headed out to my exams. I ended up doing surprisingly well.

Now begins the story in which I discovered a version of myself that I'd never met before–the version of myself I believe the voice is reminding me of by saying, "You proved to yourself many times within this particular lifetime that you could, even when you were put in situations that seemed impossible at the time."

31

Thursday night arrived, and I had one last exam on the following day. By the time I'd got home after my exams it was about 10:30 pm; I was hungry, weak and had no clue where to begin to study for my next exam. I'd had to miss class for the past month as it overlapped with another class, and when I found out, I'd had to make an uncomfortable executive decision. One class was going to take a hit, period. The question was which one? I couldn't care less about either of them, but I chose to miss the most boring one.

As I looked for my notes and collected the material I needed to go over for the exam, I looked at the clock, and I remember feeling this is absolutely impossible. It was already 11:15 pm, my exam was at 9 am the following day and I didn't know what the class was truly about. At the same time, I felt so utterly exhausted that I couldn't put a sentence together. It reached a point where I had to think about what my name was. I was in no shape to take this exam. It really wasn't going to test my intelligence at all.

I remember calling my friend and asking him what he thought was the best way to approach this. He'd been studying for that class for three days and essentially said I should play the I'm-sick card. I thought about it. But that just wasn't me. I decided to send my professor a genuine email explaining my situation and asking to write the exam maybe, at least, later in the day so I could sleep. I really needed sleep!

The professor responded with something along the lines of, "I'll be looking for you tomorrow." Talk about compassion. The truth is, I'm sure the professor had received a lot of emails like this in the past, over his years of teaching, and he might've thought I was trying to get out of the exam. He probably lumped me in with his mental image of a group of people trying to come up with an excuse.

At midnight, I was still anxious, still trying to find ways to get out of the situation and too afraid to eat or sit down because I knew I'd fall asleep. But the professor's response triggered something within me. I went from tired, weak, defeated and helpless to saying, "Okay, this charade ends right here, right now!" Suddenly, I was more aware and extremely confident. I wasn't thinking about tomorrow, or the night itself. The concept of time was no longer on my mind. I felt wired and fully plugged in, for lack of a better term. All I thought was, okay, this sucks, but let's take a look at this and see what my next steps are.

It was very clear that I couldn't study in that moment. This biological computer of mine was overheated and needed rest. I began to look at myself from a third-party perspective, which I found very interesting. I told myself that I'd give my body one sleep cycle of one-and-a-half hours–the best I could do given my situation. I planned to wake up, grab an energy bar and eat it slowly throughout whatever time I had left. I'd also buy an energy drink, but, again, I'd only take sips as needed because my body would crash otherwise.

I decided that I would turn on every single light bulb and close all the blinds to make it feel like daytime and fool my mind and body into believing it. During the summer when the sun sets late, I'm still active at night because I perceive light to be daytime, so I told myself, heck, let's trick my mind. I started to perceive myself as separate from my mind and separate from my body.

Detached from my situation and from my mind and body, I began to see clearly that my body was a sophisticated biological vehicle that allows me to experience Earth. And it had its needs. I saw my mind as a powerful tool that can be tricked to believe things that I wanted it to believe. And suddenly I had intimate knowledge of both my mind and my body. How they worked and what they needed to continue to function.

I wrote down my plan in clear, simple steps, and then I executed it. No hesitation. No worry. No fear. Nothing could stop me. Being backed up against the wall at the time, I had nothing to lose, anyway. I told myself I was simply going to do the best I could

33

with whatever time I had left. This gave me a sense of relief, as if a weight lifted off my shoulders.

I went to bed, woke up at 1:30 am, turned on every light bulb, closed the blinds, took a bite of my energy bar, a sip of my energy drink and looked at the pile of papers. As soon as I sensed that feeling of fatigue, defeat and weakness about to come up again, I reminded myself of that feeling of empowerment, and I made a quick decision—before the voice of doubt could creep up and convince me otherwise—to start with the latest material first.

The rules were simple: keep working, stay focused. If you don't understand it the first time, try it again, then move on. At 7:30 am I had no clue how so much time could've had passed. I had two double-sided papers left to go over for the exam, but I decided to rest first. I remember telling myself that I needed at least fifteen minutes to close my eyes and not to worry about waking up. Indeed, fifteen minutes later, I was up. After a quick shower, I headed out the door to my exam.

As I walked to my exam, a voice told me, "You nailed it, and you deserve to relax now. Don't think about the remaining four pages. You've really gone above and beyond, and you did your best."

Those words were music to my ears. But then, another voice came up and said, "You've worked so hard, so diligently, and now you want to give up when all you have left is four pages?"

I made it to the auditorium where the exam was being held. Everyone stood outside chatting, and there I was still debating whether or not I should go over the four pages. I stood in line, took my seat number and found my seat. While the other students walked in, I found myself getting up, walking up to my backpack and leaving the room to quickly skim through the four pages.

I remember someone throwing a comment at me: "You know what you know; last minute revising won't help."

In addition, another voice in my head said, "Your mind is

already shut down; you expect yourself to memorize this now?" This voice continued to arise, and I continued to ignore it.

The exam moderator called me as I was going through the last page. It truly felt like an uphill battle till the end.

I walked into the exam with a feeling of 'now I've done my best. Whatever happens next, I'm completely at peace with it.'

I sat and skimmed through the exam: three questions, and the last two questions weighed seventy percent of my entire grade. The last two questions were based on the material that I had just looked over before walking into the exam. Yes, the exam was based on those four pages!

I knew it in my gut! I told myself as I immediately jotted down the answers stored in my short-term memory.

A piece of me wishes it could send you the images in my head right now. What an experience it was. As I wrote down the answers, I forgot what I was writing. I could feel the information leaking out of my short-term memory. It was a fight against time. My mission was to make sure I got the answers down before I forgot all the information. After dealing with questions two and three, I went back to the first question and answered that as well. I finished the entire exam in less than an hour, and it was a three-hour exam.

While I revised my answers. I reread the second and third questions, and discovered that I did not know the answers. I read what I'd written, and I was impressed. I remember telling myself that there was no point revising the exam before handing it in, because I really didn't know the answers better than the version of me from thirty something minutes before. It was as if something came through me, did its thing and then left.

It was the same thing that nudged me to leave the room and read those four pages. I walked out that room not caring about the A I was about to get, but the process to getting it. Now that was a mind twist. That is something to ponder and celebrate. For the first time, I met this superhuman side of me who's not affected by grogginess, who's in control, in check, detached from drama, who sees the big picture and who sees things for what they really are.

When I was him—one-hundred percent in my element—everything was plain and simple. I had clarity. As if I'd put on a pair of prescription glasses that I hadn't known I needed in the first place. I learned that fear and anxiety are a choice. And most importantly, the night before my exam I would've bet every single penny I had that it was impossible to study in a matter of hours an entire semester worth of material from a class with which I'm not familiar, and then not just pass it, but ace it. I was baffled, confused and excited all at the same time.

After this recollection, I said to the voice, "I know you're listening to my thoughts. I have a question for you." With a curious and childlike tone, I asked, "Why am I not always tapped into that aspect of me that only sees what's right here, right now. That aspect of me that's not affected by 'time,' that doesn't project into the future? Clearly, I couldn't have done it without that version of me coming out. How can I always tap into that version of me? What's stopping me from being that version of me? Wait a minute ... are you the same voice I heard back then?"

I felt my heart beating fast from the excitement of remembering and beginning to understand what I'd gone through during that time in my life. And also from the possibility of finding out who this voice was! I didn't get a response from the voice, so I continued to ponder and enjoy how I felt in that moment. I gazed up at the sun and allowed it to warm my face while the water swirled around my feet.

Eventually, the voice popped up again, saying, "You are a limitless being. You don't need to find yourself in a situation where you're backed up against a wall with no other option but to surrender and give up control over what you're going through to allow me to guide you. Let me try to make this clearer for you. Remember the cartoon that covered the story of Aladdin that you used to watch when you were younger? With the genie guiding and supporting Aladdin, he begins to tap into abilities and do things that he never thought he could do before, like the dance moves he performed to impress the Princess.

"This is the same dance of trust we've talked about before, between the horse and the rider of the horse. Notice also all the good fortune that comes to Aladdin when he allows the genie to help him. Notice how the genie is comical. He takes himself lightly and faces challenges and adversity with humor. He can do the latter because he always sees life through those set of glasses that you wore that night–the ones that allow you to see things as they are. Because of that, he's able to detach from events and avoid becoming a victim of the scenarios he finds himself facing.

"This answers some of your questions. The rest will be answered in their right time. Now, I have a question for you for a change. Tell me, what does 'doing it your way' really mean to you? Does it mean you want to be a rebel? Or maybe it's this inner knowing telling you that you have a bigger purpose here, one you want and need to fulfill?"

"I don't know; that's the problem," I replied in worry.

"Or maybe it's about facing and freeing yourself from that feeling I got from you earlier, that your perception of your father was that he pushed you in order for you to succeed. But at the same time, his push wasn't necessarily aligned with what you truly wanted for yourself. And you ended up believing that a lot of what you 'must do' is based on the approval of others. And that's what you want to understand and then free yourself from," the voice said gently.

"Is that when it started for me?" I asked in a quiet voice. Then I added, "I'm sure you won't believe me, but the truth is, I don't feel that I seek the approval of others. But I trust you enough now to know that you're here to help me."

Compassionately the voice said, "Yes, dear, it was at that

37

point in your childhood that you began to subconsciously lock your-self in without even knowing it. Welcome to society. And no, getting others' approval is not something you think about all the time, but it is something that's driven inside you at a subconscious level, and that's why it's tricky. The reason why it's important for you to understand this is because it will give you a pretty good indication of who you are on a level that you're not aware of right now. Just yet.

"See ... the majority of everything that you do in your auto-matic day to day life and the decisions that you make are rooted in your subconscious beliefs–things you're not even aware of. There-fore, if you're looking to understand yourself, you want to dig deeper, and I mean deeper. How do you get there? I hate to break it to you, but there's no such thing as getting there; it's not a destination. It's not something tangible. This is a very good example of a time where you'll want to use and capitalize on some of your other gifts in conjunction with logic to solve the confusion, so to speak.

"But right here, right now. I see lines. Very straight yet equally spaced lines. This tells me that your current perception is rooted in the fact that you need facts in front of you before anything else. Well, that's one way of seeing life, I guess. But really, deep down that's your mind's way of trying to protect you. That is how you feel safe in the world. It's what you've learned to experience, based on your upbringing. Many do it, to different degrees, of course, but in return, it negates their inner feelings.

"These so-called inner feelings are subtle and cannot neces-sarily be explained solely by logic. So unconsciously you tend to steer away from trusting your feelings and emotions in order to pursue something that is much safer to you, or so you think. Remember you do have free will. You are willingly putting yourself where you are right now based on the information you've picked up on your jour-ney thus far. But it doesn't always have to be this way, right? Because you're free. I know you don't see it or feel it yet. But truly you are free."

CHAPTER 6

FAITH AND TRUST

"So you see," the voice continued, "you're dealing with this safety and security paradigm. What else? I can hear you say, 'Anxiety.' Well, anxiety is always about the future, and it's rooted in not knowing and not being able to see into the future. But tell me, can you really see what tomorrow is going to be like? Not really, right? So what happens when you go day by day, living and getting up in the morning and the world doesn't end? What happens? It becomes your norm.

"Every day you go to bed at night, and you've developed faith that you'll wake up in the morning and continue with your life. In the same way, when faith and trust in yourself become a part of your every day, they become your norm. Pretty soon the norm becomes something you do without even thinking, and then it becomes part of your developed belief system.

"In other words, in order for you to think differently and believe different things, you need to start somewhere first. You then slowly integrate the new into your daily routine. You're not going to get up tomorrow with an expectation that, all of a sudden, you're going to completely shift who you are, because if you did, you're going to end up in a mental hospital, and we don't want that, do we? I mean, imagine yourself waking up tomorrow and everything about you is different, including the fact that you can't remember who you are. How would that feel? It's confusing, borderline insanity, right?

"What I'm feeling, here, is that deep inside of you, you feel that you can't have what you want. But it's not because you can't, in the sense that you can't do it; you can't because outside influences tell you so. They limit you. That, however, is only your current perception. That's how you currently observe and interpret your world. That's not how you need to be or have to be moving forward. Now that's up to you.

"First you want to recognize what your current perception is, and it's based on your belief that you can't have and do what you want. Because if you believed that you could, then you wouldn't have anxiety. So you're basically bumping against walls, and the walls are saying, "Hey ... pay attention, pay attention, come back here."

"It's about going through the obstacles and realizing that you can have and do what you want, even though it feels quite treacherous and you can't see it just yet. In other words, a lot of what you'll develop as you go through this experience of transformation is the skill of inner trust and faith in yourself. Now that's leadership quality.

"This is how you tune into your own guidance–your intuition. A lot of it has to do with faith and trust in yourself and most importantly a belief, a belief that you can. The words faith, trust and belief here are not tied to anything, anyone or any organization, religious or otherwise, that's outside of you. I'm talking about faith, trust and belief in yourself first and foremost. Period. And you've had a taste of how powerful you become when you believe in yourself and have faith and trust that you can. Haven't you? You've done it before, dear one. You're simply gaining more awareness of experiences that you've been through. The intellect is playing catch up. That's all there is to it.

"Before I crept into your thoughts, one of the questions I posed was, 'How do I approach him, because he's one of 'those' people?' And the answer was, 'Facts ... facts ... facts. That's how you'll get to him.' They also said, 'Show him that he can versus he should or shouldn't.' If you take a step back and look at your approach to thinking, you'll conclude that a good portion of your thought process, or your approach to decision making, starts with 'should I do this?' Or 'should I do that?'

"Let me imitate you for a second and let me know how I do. Hmm ... let me think about this ... If I go down this path, then this will happen, but if I go down this other path, then this other thing will happen. Hmm ... Which path is the right path for me? I don't want to make the wrong choice. Maybe I should ask and take someone else's opinion ... and there it goes again ... suddenly you're anxious, nervous and you waste your time and energy being stuck in the mentality of right and wrong.

"It's only you who continuously paralyze yourself by your own thoughts, which you quite literally create, but they take over and shape your reality, rather than you being the one in control of your own reality. You see the irony? You create something, and then you let it control you. Well, there's more to the latter than what meets the eye, but for now, you want to free yourself from the habit pattern of the mind. Again, just in case you missed it. You want to free yourself from the habit pattern of the mind.

"Stop looking for confirmation from anyone or anything that is outside of you. Full stop. No one can and/or will ever be able to walk in your shoes. So even people who truly love you and genuinely want your best interest can't tell you what to do. The best they can do is share their perspective with you and tell you what they'd do if they were in your situation, not what you would do."

THEMINDCHEMIST

CHAPTER 7

CONFORMITY

"Let's move from here and lie down near the shallow end of the water," the voice suggested.

It sounded like a good idea, so I found a sweet spot and lay on my back in the water, staring up at the sky. I needed a break from the voice. I thought to myself that what the voice just said was very true. Up to that point, I had a very structured (right or wrong) way of seeing life. I just never sat down and asked myself where it came from or why I even have that pattern of thinking ...

The voice continued, "I'm going to shift gears now. Did you notice how when I reminded you of an experience you'd been through, although all I did was remind you of something that happened in the past, you felt the associated feelings as if it was all happening now. It's funny how that works, isn't it? To be able to re-live a memory and actually feel the exact same feeling that you felt back then, right here, right now. And it all starts with a thought. This is going to be an important tool for you to work with soon.

"I'm glad I brought it up again because we never really talked about what caused all those uncomfortable feelings to come up during

43

that time in your life. It all started when you noticed that your grades weren't reflecting your understanding of the topic. In some classes you barely passed, and all of this was new to you since you were used to getting your so-called A's back in high school, which also added to the pile of confusion.

"But soon enough you learned that the secret sauce behind getting an A wasn't studying or learning the material in the book from cover to cover. It was never fully about gaining knowledge of the material at hand but about knowing your professor. It was about identifying that there was a system, understanding how it worked and then playing it. So, you drafted your own equation with clear constants, and all you needed to figure out next was the missing variable that made that equation true, and that day it came to you clear as daylight. The missing variable was the professor.

"Now you'd found your equation, all you had to do next was plug it all back in and watch it work. You learned a valuable lesson that would shape the rest of your undergraduate degree and, indirectly and more broadly, your life experience itself. From that day forward, you made sure to know who the professor was before you took the class. What was their style of teaching? Is it easier to get an A with another professor? What was their teaching method? And most importantly only study what they wanted you to know (not what you wanted to know), and study the type of questions and tricks that that particular professor tended to ask. And if you did all of the above, you realized that you'd get an A just like that.

"Your focus became derailed from seeking the type of knowledge your inner child imagined when you first got to university. You became laser focused on the dangling carrot, this thing they called an A. That's when you subtly conformed and dropped your previous attitude–one that was full of eagerness and excitement towards learning and knowledge–just so you could bring your average GPA up and land a job that would pay you well. This is an example of what I shared with you earlier today when I told you that your focus is being steered away from finding out who you are and what's really happening in plain sight, right in front of you. You're kept busy in the subtlest of ways as you anxiously react to what you're being forced to go through–society has many different dangling carrots for you to run after.

"I know that that was clear, but I also know that you like to learn through analogies and examples. See ... It's not that different from that game of chess that you had the other day with your friend. You moved one pawn; he moved another. You moved another pawn, and he moved another, then you knocked off one of his pawns. He got slightly agitated and became laser focused, counting how many pawns he still had and comparing them to the number of pawns that you had. He was so focused on knocking off the pawn that caused him to lose his last one; that he lost the big picture. He got caught up in the game.

"While he was in that space, you were in a whole different mindset. You were completely detached from what was happening to the pawns. In fact, when you noticed his behavioral pattern, you started feeding him pawns on the opposite side to where you were planning your next move. You gave him exactly what he wanted, or what he thought he wanted, and made him happy, because he thought he was winning since he had more pawns on the chess board than you did.

"Continuing to react to your moves and seeking immediate gratification kept him happily busy. No complaints on his side. While you, on the other hand, were patiently observing the big picture and waiting for an opening to get to the king, which is what this whole game of chess is about. You were emotionally detached from what was happening to you, how many pawns you had left, or how many your opponent had left, because it didn't matter. None of it mattered. You used his reactive nature against him and gave him what he wanted until the path cleared up and you got to the king.

"You decided to go for a rematch, but this time you told him how you won the first time around and how you were intentionally giving him what he wanted and distracting him as you focused on the end goal, the end game. He looked at you and told you that he wasn't reacting, that is just his style of playing. Once he knew what you knew, he began the second game by copying your every move. You moved the pawn on the right; he moved the pawn on his right, and so on. Soon enough, he knocked off one of your pawns, and you knocked off one of his, and as soon as you felt gravitated towards reacting to his actions, you pulled back and remembered that none of it mattered; the end game is the king. His mental habit pattern got the best of him, and he went back to his reactive nature, got distracted and caught up in the game once again.

"You explained to him what had happened that time, and he reluctantly accepted to play one last time. The next time around, he was too much in his head, thinking about what you were thinking, and as such, he was far from being present. He was out of balance, and it was very easy to win again. Do you get it now? You were playing the old version of yourself. You're learning that when you identify with the game, you lose track of the big picture. That's when you get stuck in your dramas, and you begin to give your power away.

"At this point in our interaction, you're getting a clearer picture of what balance means. When you lose balance, you lose a sense of who you are and end up giving your power away. When you're in the midst of it, it doesn't seem that that's the case at all. Life–the game–seems normal. It doesn't seem like you're being distracted. Just like what happens to you as you spend time seeking an A rather than knowledge, because this is how the system works. You say to yourself, 'I need to survive, so I'm going to conform.' This is a very simple example. It's much bigger than this and potently subtle.

"Remember when I told you earlier not to take anything personal because it's much bigger than you? You're beginning to slowly recognize patterns around you–objectively without judgment–and learning not to take them as individual patterns but to take them as global patterns. When you begin to do that, you'll come into many realizations of the way certain things are run from a place of pure observance. I want you to sit down with what we just covered. There are answers buried in between the lines."

I swished my head gently from side to side in the water, feeling the cool liquid caressing my skin. I totally got what the voice meant. Clear as the water in which I lay.

"That period in your life humbled you," the voice continued after I'd had a chance to ruminate on his previous words. "Your ego was put back in its place for the first time. If you hadn't gone through that period in your life, then maybe you'd still believe that someone with a low GPA or someone who had failed a class is not smart but now, after going through this experience and being thrown off your game, so to speak, your perception changed and you learned that there is no such thing as smart. It's all just choices, decisions, experiences, and you concluded that grades were more like a measure of your conformity rather than a measure of your intelligence.

"You went through a great growth spurt during that time. You gained experiential knowledge of the concept of a system, the concept of conformity and how subtle it is, and a glimpse of what society is about. How people accept things, even if what they're doing makes no emotional sense to them, but in order to survive, they abide by the system just like you did. It was one heck of an uncomfortable experience, but the most important lesson to take away from it all was that you didn't listen to your own intuition, and you joined the herd despite every single fiber of your being telling you to trust yourself and follow your gut feeling. You got to respect the good old peer pressure technique. So subtle, yet so potent.

"Tell me. How did it make you feel, shutting down your aspirations, shutting down this energy of you and just following what the rest were doing? It wasn't fun times, was it? It was a tad dramatic–it felt like someone sucked the soul out of you, and that was when you lost that connection you once had with yourself. If Juan, the owner of that ranch, was here, he'd say that you weren't much different from one of his nine horses who'd lost connection with themselves to conformity. Yes, that was when it all started for you. That was the beginning of the separation between you and the dude inside.

"That was when you abandoned him in favor of fitting in, and that's when the pipes began to clog up, and the cell service got choppy, until eventually none of it was able to reach you, although the signals never stopped. Because, remember how your life was before all that happened to you? You were the king of your own world. You know why? Because you had balance. Why? Because you had full faith and trust in yourself and your abilities. Up until your world was turned upside down, and you started to slowly drift away from the dude inside. That's when your levels of anxiety and discomfort sky rocketed. Again, why? Because that's when you began to resist (conform), and your resistance (horse/mind) to your own intuition (rider/soul) gave birth to those uncomfortable feelings and emotions that you experienced. There you go, now you understand what happened back then.

"Like we covered before. Since no one taught you what to do with those feelings, you decided to power through it. Now, although you claim that you powered through it, really what you're saying is that you'd become good at suppressing and ignoring your emotions, so they couldn't hurt you anymore. At this point, you have accepted this about yourself, because I feel no resistance from you as I share this information with you. You're beginning to realize that you can only go so far living life that way (suppressing your emotions), before you really lose the sense of the dude inside (who you really are).

"Those who get to that point where they've lost all connectivity become so estranged from their own internal compass, their own internal guidance system, that they genuinely begin to believe that what they do is who they are. And that's when you begin to identify yourself with what you do, which is the reason why you feel lost. Because without your internal guidance system, it's hard to see that it's about who you are, not what you do, and what you do is not who you are."

CHAPTER 8

IDENTITY CRISIS

I asked the voice, "If I understand you right, then you're saying that I'm dealing with an identity crisis. Is that what you're saying?"

"Yes. In a way you are dealing with an identity crisis. Up until now your identity has been based on what you've been able to collect from outside you. Is it not? And I'm telling you that it's time for you to redefine your own identity in a much greater sense. And to do it fearlessly with a whole lot of humor. I know it feels uncomfortable, but it truly is time for you to radically change your views about yourself. To bust down boundaries and rise out of the grogginess and the pettiness of day-to-day dramas and begin to connect with others on a universal and more inclusive scale." said the voice with a sigh.

He then said, "For you to be able to understand your identity, you want to move away from defining yourself. See ... when you make a statement and a definition of who you think you are, you create a boundary. An imaginary wall immediately goes up all around you when you define yourself. The more you define yourself, the more limitations you create as far as what you think you're capable of experiencing. Yes. Listen to yourself as you speak. Notice how you speak your own parameters to the world. You and many others describe yourselves so well that you form other people's boundaries around yourself.

"You say, 'Hi. I'm so-and-so. I've collected so-and-so letters after my name, and please don't forget to call me by the prefixes I've collected before my name, as well. And I'm from so-and-so...' and it continues. You spend most of your time labelling and defining yourself and anything that's not you as separate from you to emphasise how awesome you are. Why? Because you think that that makes you eloquent and refined. You think you're sculpting this magnificent statue, when, in reality, all you're doing is separating yourself from whoever you're speaking to.

"You then seek education, which is all malarkey, and you think that the more technical your degree is and the more A's you get, the more knowledgeable you are. Should I laugh or are you already laughing at this? I know, it's hilarious. So you see, the more you define, the more you separate yourself, the more rigid your character (your ego) becomes. That's why there's a lot for you to overcome.

"The issue is not with ego. Many demonize ego and say it's wrong and must go away. Yes, ego can be sneaky at times and loves attention, but that doesn't make ego evil. Ego is nothing but the character you portray, and it's a natural part of your human experience. Ego serves you in some ways. It only gets distorted or imbalanced when you identify with it and believe it's what and who you are. This is the identity crisis we're talking about. That's what you're beginning to understand and learning to overcome as you move from the world of thinking into the world of perceiving.

"Like I said before, you're in a restructuring period. What you're working towards right now is renouncing control of your identity and allowing it to have a whole new structure. A new definition. It's a very subtle energy, this redefining of who the self is. I want you to listen to this carefully: as you redefine your identity, you'll not become less and you'll not lose a thing. In fact, you'll gain perspective on yourself. This is what you're having a hard time convincing yourself of. Why? Because the logical mind has convinced you that you could lose yourself. That's why you had this sense of powerlessness when you let go of your job, the money and all that built up your character (ego) at the time.

"You're simply ready to give birth to another character, a character that is more aligned with your authentic self and truest desires. Exciting times! Really though, it is exciting. It's all shifting and changing for you. You've come far in such a short period of time. You're in the process of taking your power back, and in the meantime, you're being polished and prepared for your next role.

"Remember ... all these experiences are happening for you; don't adopt that victim mentality that has plagued those around you and think that life is happening to you. Don't engage in finger pointing, but rather try to understand why you feel the way you do and the role the other person played that brought about the feeling. Those who are involved in dramas and play victims are so out of touch with their own feelings that they don't connect how they feel with what they're thinking.

"At the end of the day, you are a result of your thoughts. If there's nothing else you'll take away from today's conversation, you'll learn that your thoughts formulate your world. No matter what situation you find yourself experiencing–comfortable or not–know that it's there to teach you something new. It's there to help you grow and set you up for what's yet to come. With that in mind, you can now approach your experiences with a bird's eye view, filled with curiosity as to what you're supposed to learn from what you're going through. No more being sucked into the experience and losing track of the big picture.

"Just like that game of chess. You're learning that when you're caught up by your circumstances, generally your first response is to contract and push back. This is because you're getting consumed by the event by looking too closely at it and not expanding your vision to take in the bigger picture. You want to allow yourself to step outside the scenario you're enacting, observe it and see what it's doing for you, and then learn from it.

"No need to forget a 'bad' experience. I want you to hear this carefully: you do yourself a great disservice when you seek to forget a 'bad' experience. Information in that experience can teach you more about yourself. When you disengage from the event bringing about any type of emotion, it makes it easier for you to understand what that emotion is trying to tell you and teach you. The less you identify with the character you're playing, the easier life gets because it gets easier to detach from dramas.

"As soon as you get less attached to the dramas, you'll not feel so caught up and victimized by them or your opponent. You'll learn to appreciate and be grateful for your opponent, for they're playing a crucial part in your personal growth. I know it's much easier said than done, but eventually you'll find yourself no longer in reactive mode and no longer a victim to your mind's knee-jerk reactions, which tend to be impulsive, defensive and automatic in nature.

"You'll learn to tame that poor little mind chap of yours, who's full of fear, and show him that there's more to it all–just like taming that wild horse. Love him, thank him and tell him that it's okay not to have all the answers. Re-introduce him to the dude inside. Re-introduce him to you, and show him that he's not in it alone. Show him that he has nothing to be afraid of. Show him that there's no need to go into panic-attack mode when change comes knocking on the door."

CHAPTER 9

CHANGE

The voice continued, "Tell that little chap the truth. Tell him that change is his bestie. Change is like that real friend who keeps it one hundo and is always challenging you to stretch your comfort zone and reach higher. Yes, it's true, with change comes uncertainty, and it's normal to feel some fear. But there's no need to let that fear take over and decide to take on Mr. Change in the boxing ring just because the mind, in its current state of understanding, simply cannot conceptualize and understand this change all by itself.

"That's why you have Mr. Intuition. Mr. Intuition is here to help the mind navigate through uncertainty. Keep reminding him that he's not alone. He's got help if he can only get himself into a more receptive state, to allow help to come in. But what's also fueling the resistance to change besides uncertainty? It's all the time, effort, commitment and dedication that comes along with it. Let's keep it real; it's a lot of hard work, and the poor mind is already depleted and overwhelmed from all the responsibilities of the hectic working day.

"And now you're introducing more new information (change) for the mind to chew on and consider, on top of its saturated and overflowing cup of should do's, must do's and have to's. Can you blame the dude for being reactive and resisting it all?

"Change is best when it comes from the inside rather from the outside. In other words, you want to have the flexibility to change; you want to be able to give up old behavior patterns that no longer serve you–without too much thought–so you can move forward into what you call the future with ease. I know it's difficult sometimes to move out of old places you've lived in. Because it seems as if they've become your identity. It's very important for you to understand this because you're on the verge of a leap of consciousness, and I've been holding your hands for quite a while now. I'm pushing your paradigms. I'm stretching your identity because I'm preparing you for your next adventure. As you integrate and realize what this change means, it will alter you inside out.

"Change means realignment; change means many things will be coming apart in your life and many other things will be coming together as you develop trust. Don't resist it. It's here to help you. Yes, I know it's not necessarily smooth at the moment. It's always challenging to integrate change in its early stages. I know you're concerned about the changes occurring within yourself as well as on the globe, but allow yourself not to continually project yourself in anticipation of what lies ahead.

"All that exists is here in your present moment of experience, and this moment will continue to unfold into future moments that maybe hold answers to questions from your present. You see? Past, present, future, it's all here in this moment. The logical mind detests what I just told you because it's always wanting control. As long as it remains untamed, it will always hold you in limitation and give you a sense of false security and a false sense of identity, as we have already established.

"This takes me to the real practical question of where do you start? And how do you unclog the pipes we've talked about so you can avoid turning into one of Juan's horses? It all begins with the mind. The work you're here to do is work within your mind. The first step is acknowledging what we've already talked about and then being willing to get over your self-pity, be willing to face change and stop allowing yourself to become a victim of fear.

"Stop being a victim in situations where you diminish yourself and refuse to stand up to what you know is right for you and say, 'I don't like this.' Don't dim your light any longer, and stop doing things that you don't like doing. It doesn't mean you have to be angry about it and rebel. Not at all. You simply begin to stand up for the integrity of your being. From there you roll up your sleeves for once and be prepared to get your hands dirty. I mean reaaal dirty. I want you to imagine your entire arms reaching deep down some sewage line and you being totally okay with it.

"Once you've reached that state of mind, from there you don't have to do anything. Well, you don't have to do anything physically or anything that's outside of you. What I'm saying is that your last step is simply to get out of your own way. In your case, the reason why the process was smooth is because you simply went with the flow of your body. Your body needed movement, so you decided to get back in shape and play soccer again. Did you notice what I just said? I said you decided to play again. I wanted you to pay attention to that because I want to emphasize the importance of play in your life.

"Inject more playfulness into your life. When you play, you get yourself out of the logical mind and allow yourself to move beyond that boundary, that limitation, and tap into the creative mind. When you play, you allow yourself to tap into the child within, who's not arguing to be right. You tap into that impulsive self, that's uninhibited, and that intuitive self has a direct pipeline to them. That's when you begin to create with ease and with all the fun, joy and harmony you could possibly want. Play allows you to let go and terminate many of the contracts you have with the logical mind or the ego. These limit you; they inhibit you because of their fear of being wrong.

"Went on a tangent right there. Where were we again? ... Oh right ... We were talking about soccer. So after you started playing soccer again, your body asked for more, and suddenly, one day, you found yourself practicing yoga (asana). You unconsciously moved away from certain foods, certain drinks, certain people, certain patterns of behaviour ... Dude, I know you don't know it—at a conscious level—but you were literally listening to your body. And because of that, you saved up all that energy that would've otherwise been spent on overcoming the resistance and stubbornness of the logical mind as it tried to rationalize and make sense of it all. You learned that the very aspect of trying limits you. The trying is what makes it hard. Simply being right here, right now, is by its very definition, freeing.

"When you're free, you'll come to understand and feel that your abilities truly are limitless, and they go way beyond what you think is possible. And by the way, I keep using the word 'unknowingly' or 'unconsciously' to emphasise how smooth the process can be if you just get yourself in a receptive state and allow it all to happen without the need to know the how. Because the how is not always a logical thing, dear one.

"As you've experienced yourself, you had no idea what was happening behind the scenes or that you were allowing it all to happen. You simply found yourself doing something that you enjoyed doing, which was, at the same time, tuning you into the now. When it was time to dive slightly deeper into the other clogged parts of the pipes, you suddenly found yourself exposed to yet another experience that would set you up for what you needed at the time, which was Vipassana. Just. Like. That.

"Which is why I said that all your experiences are happening for you, not to you—and that there're no such thing as coincidences or lucky chances. They're all cooperative incidences planned and designed for you. You didn't plan any of it, did you? The only thing you did was get out of your own way and not fight the urge or challenge the 'why' behind all of it. You just did it. You skipped the trying part and went straight into it. This is a great achievement for someone who's painfully analytical and has been hardened to ignore feelings and solely follow logic and fear-based practicality. I salute you for it."

I understood what he was saying, but part of me wondered exactly how it all worked.

The voice responded to my query without me verbalising it. "Funny. We just went over the 'how' using your own personal experience. The mind ... what a creature. Back and forth, back and forth ... but I want to double click on the fact—because I know you love facts—that you were doing it without having the knowledge of the 'how.'

"There's your proof that you don't need to know the 'how.' But an aspect of you doesn't believe that the 'how' isn't always a logical thing. And because of that, every time the input it receives is not something tangible or something that it has knowledge of or is capable of rationalizing, it gets all worked up. And it's not because that aspect of you is up to no good; it's just that it wants to be right and the reason why it wants to be right is because it's afraid. And all the way deep down there, what's really fueling all of this is its need to feel safe and in control. It's as simple as that. But, hey, who am I to tell all of this. You've deduced and experienced all this through the many hours and days of meditation."

CHAPTER 10

VIEWING OF THE SELF

The voice was on a roll; he didn't even stop for a second. "It's safe to say that it was in your first Vipassana course that you met your mind for the first time. Now, let's keep it real; that experience was a mind twist from the very beginning. When you entered that registration area and were asked to fill out some paperwork and then surrender your possessions into a plastic bag, it felt like you were admitting yourself into jail.

"But then, soon enough, it all started. Complete silence. No words, no sound, no physical exercise to let it all out, no contact whatsoever, yes, not even eye contact. No electronics. No books. No writing. For the first time in your life, you found yourself in an environment where you had no external influences bombarding you and trying to peer into your mind and persuade you to go one way or the other.

"You, yourself and you for ten days, the duration of the course. The first thing you were instructed to do on your first day was to sit on your ass, focus on your breath and feel the sensation caused by your breath in the area between your nostrils and upper lip. Those were the simple instructions. You sat down in that meditation hall, you closed your eyes and you said to yourself this is going to be easy peasy.

"Before long you began to experience pain in your lower back, and that distracted you from focusing on your breath. Next, you found yourself remembering random moments from the past, moments that you'd shared with people, times from your childhood, conversations with your parents, all just passing by.

"Thoughts about what you wanted to do next with your life bubbled up, and you started to think about that trip you had planned to Peru right after the course. And then suddenly you found yourself all the way back in high school remembering that time when you and your friends stayed up all night cracking jokes 'til the break of dawn. You decided to stay there, and even cracked a quiet laugh as you relived that good time.

"You felt those pleasant emotions as if they were happening right then and there. The experience felt so good that it made you desire it more. So you went even deeper into it and could even hear the music that was playing in the background when you guys were hanging out. It just kept on getting better and better. The more you stayed there, the more real it felt, as if you'd literally travelled back in time.

"It felt so pleasurable and satisfying that you wanted to stay there, but then, all of a sudden, it all just vanished. Just like that. The whole experience disappeared, evaporated with no notice or warning. One moment you were in a happy place and the following moment you found yourself back in that meditation hall with that aggravating lower back pain.

"You were left only with that feeling of withdrawal, and all you wanted to do next was go back there, back to that space. You craved how that memory made you feel so much that you spent the next little while with eyes closed focusing on going back there, but it didn't work. Instead you amplified that back pain again ... and that made you agitated and angry. Why? Because you weren't getting what you wanted, and to top it all off, you started feeling pain around your hip area.

"That was when you opened your eyes and thoughts of leaving that place bubbled up. You were disappointed in yourself because you realized that this whole time you hadn't been doing the one simple thing you were asked to do—focus on your breath. You, being someone who has high expectations of themselves, got yourself all flustered and started beating yourself up for not being able to focus on your breath.

"The following day you were the first person in that meditation hall. With determination, you sat down and closed your eyes again, and not too long after, something magical happened, didn't it? It all clicked and came together. You realised that the reason why you were angry and hard on yourself the day before wasn't truly about you having high expectations of yourself. It was way deeper than that.

"You understood that your reaction was ultimately another excuse triggered by your mind/ego as a defense mechanism to protect itself from what it doesn't understand and doesn't want to accept. What happened there was that one aspect of your ego resisted accepting what another aspect of your ego had concluded about yourself. And that is that you didn't have full control of your own thoughts like you originally thought and believed you did.

"That realization that was buried deep down in the vast stillness of your very center, past the surface waves of the egoic mind, and through your emotional undercurrents, it shook your entire belief system. It shook your entire world. No wonder your ego didn't want to accept the truth and decided to resist and go into panic attack mode. If it didn't have full control over its own thoughts that meant it didn't know everything. Which meant that it was wrong about itself, which triggered doubt, and from there it spiraled down to, could it be that I've been wrong my entire life? What else was I wrong about? And the spiral downwards continued.

63

"Your mind at the time was wired to see things in black and white, and so it adopted the belief that there is such a thing as being right or being wrong, when in reality, life is in between. Which goes back to what we were talking about earlier and that's to walk down the middle lane and not to be influenced to favoring one way of seeing life over the other. Because like we established earlier, that's when you begin to give power to something outside of you.

"See ... every time you allow yourself to give your power to something that is outside of you, you become out of balance and feel that you're not in control. Just like your chess opponent. When they played you the third time, they were too into their head and thinking about what you were thinking and lost their balance, which made it very easy for you to win. Out of balance. That's exactly what was happening back there in that meditation hall.

"If you haven't noticed, it was all about you being right or wrong. Being right was translated to being safe, and being wrong was translated to not being safe. But I'm going to let you in on a little secret–don't tell anyone–there is no right or wrong when it comes to your life and what you want to do. It's all just experiences that are there to teach you and empower you through experiential knowledge. This is your school. Life itself is the school. Your experiences are your hands-on, project-based classes, and you are both the student and the teacher.

"Life wants you to be more knowledgeable. Life is wanting to widen your vision, not narrow it down. It wants to remind you of all the power that you have within. It's not wanting to take it away by compartmentalizing, separating and isolating information so that you can only see a portion of the truth. Rather it's teaching you to explore more and be more open so you can finally understand and see the big picture and how it's all connected together."

I pulled myself up out of the water and found a spot to sit on the edge of the shallows. Once comfortable, I said, "That makes a lot of sense. There is, however, one concept that's confusing me. When you said there's no right or wrong. What did you mean exactly? That I can just go and do whatever I want? Even if it's a harmful act? That doesn't feel right to me."

"Oh, dear one. Don't even go there. When your feeling center opens, such thoughts won't even cross your mind. Because when your feeling center opens, you're connected to how someone else is. You would feel their pain and won't have it in you to harm another soul. Conflict and war occur when feeling centers are shut down. Yes, many have their feeling centers shut down. No one taught them how to open their feeling centers. But this won't last for long dear one. Not for long ...

"But to answer your question. I meant that the anger that you were experiencing back in that meditation hall was only your judgment, anyway. Like I said, you love to call yourself right or wrong. Why? Because most of the time you want to be accepted. You feel that no one will like you if you do this or that. You feel that no one will like you if you feel this way or if you feel that way. So what do you end up doing? You end up not giving yourself permission to have certain feelings.

"That's where the anger comes from. From suppressing yourself. You made the anger when you sat in that meditation hall all by yourself. I want you to realize that you tend to make the anger because you make judgments about what you can and cannot do. You make judgments about what is right or wrong. As such, you don't give yourself permission to feel. If you don't give yourself permission to feel, it makes the learning process much harder.

"In order for you to have information being revealed to you– as a frequency–you want to move out of right and wrong. You want to move out of judgment. The further you remove yourself from the frequency of judgment and into the frequency of acceptance, the more you allow yourself to heal, gather more information, and ultimately become more compassionate towards others. First, you're learning to be more compassionate with yourself. Relinquishing the judgment of right or wrong allows you to move through the experience and have compassion for your own self. You are learning that you ultimately desire experience and that when you judge, you miss out on the larger story. When you judge, you allow limitations to set barriers around your experience."

"Wow. Gotcha. Now that makes a lot of sense," I said.

The voice responded quickly, "Welcome to the dilemma of getting to know one's self. It comes with developing self-awareness, and we don't always like what we see about ourselves. Now you can understand that it was only you, and no one else, who threw you out of balance. By your own thoughts, your own judgments, your own labels, and your own need to be right–which ultimately triggered you to give your power away."

"I want to release judgment," I said, "but I don't know how."

With a cheerful tone the voice said, "It's much easier than you think. You look at your own life, and you simply become sick and tired of being judged. Then you understand that if you judge others, then you're being judged. With this knowing, you understand that your experience is mirroring to you what you do. In other words, if you're passing judgement on others, as far as what they should be doing, whether it be right or wrong according to you, then others would do the same to you in your own life. How to stop it? Like I said, you get sick and tired of being judged by others, so you simply stop doing it. Just like quitting cigarettes. How do you quit cigarettes? You simply cut it off.

"Now you have experiential knowledge of the fact that if you feel out of balance, it means you're giving your power away to someone or something outside of you. And let's be honest, realizing that you were not really in control of your own thoughts was a hard pill to swallow. But in that exact moment, when you got your epiphany and accepted the truth about yourself, pure and utter peace and relief filled you. It was as if someone took a massive load off your shoulders, a load that acted as a barrier, separating two broken pieces of you from one another. With that barrier gone, they reconnected back together. It felt like nothing you've experienced before, yet, at the same time, it was a familiar feeling that you just couldn't put a finger on.

"That was when you faced your fear, a fear that you weren't necessarily aware of. That was when you accepted that portion of yourself that you were unconsciously running away from. That was when you moved out of judgment and into the freedom of self. Into the moment, without defining any limitations, any boundaries and without having expectations as to what you think you should/ shouldn't, must/mustn't, can/cannot do or feel.

"That day, you learned that one of the best ways to overcome fear is to acknowledge it. Where you trick yourself is when you try to pretend that you're not afraid. You hold on and hide deep inside your being this intimate feeling that you'll not admit because you think it's a weakness. When you lay it out in front of you and say 'I am afraid,' you're facing the issue; you're asking to understand this fear, and you're asking for help.

"That was when the healing process kicked off. It was a rough take off for the ego, but chastened by what you'd learned about your-self, you went back to focusing on your breath again—this time with a humbled and broader perspective, and a fresher state of mind. Suddenly, those expectations of yourself were gone. You relaxed more into your feelings and away from judgment, and you made a genuine intention to let go of what you thought you knew and became ready to receive, allow and surrender.

"As the days passed and you started to practice the actual Vipassana technique itself, you learned to take away your mental interpretation and the label you assigned to your experiences. You were able to meet the sensations on your body as they were, without trying to change anything, without trying to get rid of them, without trying to become anything or expecting anything from the moment. Just very gently letting go. The deeper you dropped into your practice, the more you realized that you were ultimately there to clean house. That is, ultimately, what that whole process was about. Cleaning house. Becoming nobody.

"It was about sitting on your ass, closing your eyes and doing nothing. Like I said before, you don't need to do anything physically. The work that you're here to do is work within your mind, within the framework of your thoughts. Once you get yourself in the right mindset, once you get yourself in receptivity, all you have to do next is get out of your own way. In time when you least expect it, all that you have locked away or that you haven't dealt with over the years, will come smacking you in the face.

"Think of it this way. What happens when you don't feed your body? It begins to consume whatever source of energy it can get its hands on. When that's all consumed, your body will literally cannibalize itself. In a way, you're doing the same thing to your mind. While you're practicing Vipassana, you're starving the mind by scanning your body, paying attention to sensations, and observing them instead of reacting to them. By doing that, you're not generating any new cravings or aversions. You're not feeding the mind anymore. As such, it begins to look for food (thoughts) and that's why slowly but surely, all that you haven't dealt with over the years will surface up. When that happens, your only job is to be aware and observe it all, and stay ... yes, you guessed it ... balanced. Not to react to any of it. That was the challenge itself: not to react, not to feed the habit pattern of the mind.

"You realized that, over the years, you've innocently made up and built up layers of yourself, and you've ignorantly covered it over, over and over again. That was when you began to work on the ego selves and all your defence and protection mechanisms. These defence mechanisms can be many layered–the fierce judge, the victim, the martyr, the pleaser and that achiever dude. For the most part, these ego defences are bound up with other people's energy which amplify their effect on you.

"Through those many hours of meditation, you were draining other people's energy from your body. You were pulling out the egoic energetic systems of your parents, authority figures, culture and more. You were releasing all the conditioning and ego patterns that sabotage you and hold you in a very tight familiarity zone, and you were opening up and showing those parts of you that reality is a much broader mission.

"As you continue to grow and come to these understandings, you'll break through the layers of yourself that have held you down. Your time there was about you coming back to self. It was about you going through and examining and letting go of the many layers that you've accumulated in time. That was the beginning of the viewing of yourself without judging what comes up. That was when you began to enjoy the process. That was when you started to understand that this experience, and the journey you're on, ultimately has one overarching purpose, and that's the purpose of greater self-exploration."

CHAPTER 11

ESCAPING TIME

The voice left and I had some time to process all that he'd shared with me. At that point, I'd picked up on his style. He didn't give notice when he was about to give me a download or when he was about to leave. He just came and went. One minute he was there. The other, he was gone. Just like a choppy signal.

It wasn't long before he came back to me saying, "Your feet are getting all pruney from spending all this time in water. Let's get out and continue walking."

I looked down at my feet. He was right, of course. My feet were all crinkly and puckered, so I pulled them from the water, stood and found my clothes. I dried my feet with my T-shirt before sliding them into my Crocs, then I pulled on my T-shirt and carried on down the path. My shorts had mostly dried in the heat, and the remaining dampness in them and my T-shirt cooled my skin pleasantly as I walked.

I'd only taken a few steps before the voice continued, "We went on one of our tangents back there. But do you understand now? Back in that meditation hall when you found yourself suddenly

71

swimming in that vast flow of thoughts between past, future, past, future, those thoughts took you away from that room. They took you away from what you were doing. Remember when I mentioned early on in our conversation that where your thoughts go, your energy follows? Well, there you go, just a small example from your own experience.

"None of those things were actually happening in that moment while you sat there in that hall. Yet your energy was everywhere. Why? Because your thoughts were everywhere. They pulled you in all sorts of directions, which made you feel both physically and mentally exhausted. As if you were out all day and now you wanted to rest your mind. But tell me; what else can you do to rest? You were already literally sitting down on your ass and doing nothing, surrounded by complete silence. 'It's going to be easy peasy,' you said, eh?

"As you continued to sharpen the mind, you found yourself, at times, fully immersed and deep into your meditation. In those moments, you were able to experience what it felt like to truly be in the present. To simply drop into being. I know you've only experienced this knowledge for a few fleeting moments; but experiential knowledge of this, even if it was brief, was enough to give you a taste of what a freeing experience is truly like.

"A taste of what that horse felt when it finally surrendered all the 'thinking' that came behind the decision-making process onto you. This is what you're working towards: gifting yourself the present and freeing yourself from the habit pattern of the mind. Those wonderful moments made you feel and realize that the whole of time existed in those moments. In those moments where you were present, time wasn't a factor. In the sense that you didn't feel like you were racing against time anymore.

"See ... time doesn't really go anywhere. It's always there. It simply holds events separate from one another, that's it. And by doing

72

so, it creates what you call your past and what you call your future. It's no secret that a good chunk of your life is governed by time, but it's really interesting to understand how it works.

"A big portion of the habit pattern of the mind is to race against time. Running from one meeting to another, from one task to another, from one obligation to another. Although the aforementioned events hold true, but by understanding time and changing your perspective of it, the day flows much easier. Why? Because you begin to focus in the moment right here, right now, and then this whole being in the present thing makes a lot of sense.

"Essentially what I'm saying is this: being in the present moment allows you to escape time. Like we established, time simply holds events separate, giving birth to past and future. It acts like a knife, so to speak. If you are fully in the present moment, right here, right now, then time (aka knife) has nothing to cut. It's like you're dodging the knife at every moment.

"I'll clarify this. Let's assume that you're wanting to create a nice video. You begin by creating the content, and then when you get to the editing part of the video, you check the timeline at the bottom of the video editor's screen. You can then cut the video at certain times and end up with a collection of shorter video clips instead of one longer one.

"The events you've cut into different clips become separate, and you then label them in order to be able to reference them. Then you can shuffle and place them in whatever sequence you want within the video editor. Heck, you can even go back in time to different time frames and re-watch whatever portion of the video you feel like watching again in real-time.

"So you see, for the dude with the mouse cursor hovering over the video editor software and looking at the screen, it's all–past, present and future–happening now. So although past, present and future feel very real to the character inside the video you're watching.

To the observer of the screen, time isn't linear, is it? He's looking at all of it in real time. Here's the twist; you are both the character and the observer. Don't try to think about what I just said. Simply feel it, and later on today, it will sink in fully.

"Yes, this is similar to when you found yourself suddenly swimming in that vast flow of thoughts between past, future, past, future ... back in that meditation hall. Who was the one watching those thoughts come and go? They're asking me not to go on one of my tangents again, so we'll go over who's watching the thoughts later on. But for now, can you see that time is not so linear?

"I have to be honest with you, I'm having a hard time figuring out how to take what you just said and make it tangible in my day to day life." I responded candidly.

"I know. It's very tricky, because it seems that time governs your life. It seems that everything takes time and that you don't have time to do what you want to do. So you end up not bothering to do it because you trick yourself into thinking that 'you don't have time' to do it or you 'can't' do it. Time is not going anywhere. And if you're in the present moment, right here, right now, doing what you want to do, then time doesn't affect you.

"Time only affects you when you begin to project into the future and dwell in the past. Meaning that it affects you when you allow yourself to be sucked into the character in that video-editor software, the one whose life feels like its governed by time. Let me give you an example of this:

"You look to yourself and you say, 'Okay, I want to inject a mindful practice into my every day to help me tune into my present moment.' You say, 'Alright, starting tomorrow morning'–aka not now–'I'm going to wake up, and I'm going to meditate for twenty minutes. I'm going to do it once again before I go to bed. I'm going to do this every day! Yay!'

"You'd do very well with this for a week or so and then one day, you wake up feeling groggy and tell yourself, 'It's okay, I'll make up for it later on tonight.' Then when it's bedtime you say, 'Oh gosh, it's too late now. I don't have time'–although it's always there–'because I need to wake up really early tomorrow morning. Oh well ... I guess I can do it tomorrow morning.'

"So you see, next time, just do what you want immediately in that exact moment. There's no need to contemplate about whether or not you'll be able to wake up early tomorrow morning. Tomorrow morning? Tomorrow doesn't exist. Forget about this idea of 'Let me see now. If I went to bed at twelve o'clock at night and got up at five in the morning, that means five hours instead of eight hours of sleep, so I'm going to be three hours deficient all-day long tomorrow, so ... argh.'

"When you learn to meditate and get quiet and get peaceful, you can always fit in twenty minutes of meditation, any time during the day, and get the equivalent of a full night's sleep. Because you allow this 'time' to run your life, you miss the essence of who you are in the moment. Why? Because you're so caught up in 'time' and the 'clock' and 'yesterday' and 'tomorrow' that you're not aware of you. It's not about time at all; it's about the feeling of who you are, right here, right now, in this moment.

"No, it's not necessarily a logical thing. Meaning, okay, I'm going to roll up my sleeves now and focus on being right here, right now. It's about intending that it becomes a portion of your being. Just like sleeping, waking up, eating, etcetera. When you go to bed, you say, 'I'm going to sleep now'–you intend it–and soon enough, you fall asleep. You've done it for many years on a regular basis, so now it's a portion of you. It's that simple. Remember, intention is subtler than thought. It's through your intention that you steer energy. But more about intention later.

"What's also awesome about living in the now? That's when the genius comes out. Now you understand what happened that night

75

back at university during your final exams period. It felt impossible to accomplish what you needed to accomplish because your mind was stuck in this time thing–contemplating if you had enough time to sleep and study before your exam. You spent almost an hour just thinking and worrying until you were overwhelmed. Without knowing what you were doing back then, you just surrendered to it. You felt that the only option you had was to simply do the best you could with whatever time you had left before the exam.

"In that mindset, you escaped time. The genius came out, and he felt no fear. To him, time was no factor. There was complete attention in the moment. By doing that, you didn't spend time thinking about the situation, trying to rationalize it and calculate and measure if you had enough time. Instead, in that moment when you firmly told yourself that you were going to do the best that you could right then and there, you became the perceiver of the event that you were going through and you harnessed all that energy that would've been dissipated on trying to rationalize and calculate your way through.

"The perceiver is genius! Why? He's not tied to the event or emotionally attached to any of it. He's simply observing the character in the video-editor software. And because of that, he can see clearly and knows exactly what needs to be done. One moment unfolded into another and boom it was 7:30 am. Time? Who dat? So can you see what this whole being in the now is all about? It's only in the now that you can tap into a higher intelligence and allow yourself to be guided. Remember: to the genius within, all of time is here and now.

"And yes, that's why you give others good advice, but when it comes to you, you seek advice from others. It's because you're emotionally detached from what's happening to the other person, so you can think clearly. By becoming the perceiver of the event that you're going through, you can now begin to give yourself good advice. Why? Because you won't be emotionally attached to what the character is going through."

76

I stopped walking and shook my head in awe. "You're really good at making me understand abstract concepts, but I do have a couple of questions. Is the perceiver dude, the same dude who's watching the video editor screen back in your example? And in those moments where I felt freedom, yes, time was non-existent, but thoughts, too, were non-existent. There was nothingness. Could it be that thought and time are interconnected somehow?"

CHAPTER 12

A QUIET MIND

The voice came back to me, and I could feel his joy. "Yes! The perceiver is the same dude who's watching the video-editor screen back in that example. Now you're truly understanding what I meant when we went over your Vipassana experience and I told you, 'That was the beginning of the viewing of yourself–becoming the perceiver of your experience–without under any circumstance judging what's coming up.'

"And yes! You're learning that thought and time are strongly interconnected. You're learning that thought creates and what happens if you don't consciously create–meaning you don't deliberately add new content to the video. You'll end up automatically creating more of the same content as before. Why? Because you'll end up reusing and stealing content from what you call 'past' just to keep your video going. Again, why? Because you're constantly branching off from your thoughts, off from your existing bank of knowledge that you've accumulated thus far."

The voice paused, and I said with a contemplative tone, "Hmm ... It seems to me that thought is eternal ... Is it not?"

"It seems as if that's the case, doesn't it?" the voice replied, and then continued, "Let's look into this together. But before we do, to explore anything with such depth, you need to be free. What do I mean by free? I mean you need to gift yourself the freedom to examine what you're looking at without any distortion or bias. Without any preconceived image you have that may be based on what you think you know—that is, all the knowledge that you've accumulated up until this moment. In other words, to allow yourself to explore through a child's fresh and curious eyes ... Are you following?"

"I'm following you so far," I replied, then hesitated before adding, "What you're saying makes sense." Although it did make sense, I didn't know how to do it or if it was even possible not to allow what I knew to distort what I was looking at. I asked the voice to continue, hoping he'd answer my thoughts in his next words.

"I bring this up," the voice said, "because as you learn to examine yourself, it's important to feel free, to be able to ask yourself a question without being attached to the answer, without being biased towards what you already know. Rather to ask the question whilst being free from the answer. That type of mind is a quiet mind, and that type of mind is what you've started to experience back in that meditation hall when you surrendered. You let go of what you thought you knew and all the thoughts that made up who you are, and you said, 'I don't know.' That was when you let go of expectations from your experience. In that state of being, there was no effort or time spent searching for the answer. The quality of your thinking shifted when you actually said, 'I don't know,' and you stopped running after answers. Meaning, the latter act was you letting go of distortion. Remember how that felt when you said, 'I don't know,' and you simply let go and surrendered?"

"Yeah, I felt a sense of relief. That was also when I tapped into many self-realizations," I replied, fully in tune with the voice's words, knowing that he'd just answered my thoughts.

"Exactly, that's when you gave yourself the freedom to observe what is. When you were capable of letting go of previous knowledge and experiences and said, 'I don't know.' Although it was frightening for the ego, that's when you actually started to meditate. Remember? Your real meditation practice started the following day at 4:00 am when you began to understand what happened the day before and accepted that portion of you that was afraid of being wrong. We won't go over it again. I keep reminding you of all of this, because you ask me questions as if you believe you don't have the answers. Yet every single time, the answer lay within. It's just a matter of being fully attentive."

"Wow," I said in awe. "It just clicked. So this meditation thing is not necessarily about being seated in a cross-legged position in a meditation hall. It's the act of allowing myself to be free to examine myself attentively without any effort, without any expectation from my experience, without any preconceived image of what I think I know, or how I think I should be; rather to simply attentively observe what is ..."

I took some time to sit with that realization as I continued to walk down the path. I slowed my pace and found myself laughing at myself, because it's all so simple yet complex at the same time. One moment it's all as clear as day light. In another moment it's all foggy again. But the words present and be were making more and more logical sense to me.

The voice returned, saying, "Going back to your question on thought. If you look at your question with a quiet mind, you can see that you already know the answer.

"What were you doing in that mediation hall? You were observing sensations, but you also indirectly began to observe your thoughts moving: arising and passing away. You noticed how those thoughts created images (memories) in your head, and if you liked the image, you wanted to stay there, and if you didn't, you wanted to get rid of it. Your desire, which now you can see clearly, is a product of sensation and the thoughts that accompany that sensation–thoughts that take you one way or the other. By learning, back in that meditation hall, how not to react to what comes your way, you were learning to transcend this cycle of craving and aversion.

"Now, the more you relaxed into your beingness, the more you began to simply observe how the thought came without naming it or labeling it and without creating an image. You practiced being attentive, like a surgeon in the middle of an operation, and using all your energy to watch what is without allowing your memory to intervene. You simply observed what is. Are you still with me?"

"Absolutely ... Keep going ... Don't stop!" I said whilst being afraid I'd lose my attention.

"In that state of attentiveness, just like that surgeon who's very present, thought does come to an end. Time, too, comes to an end," the voice responded softly, yet firmly.

"Oh! That's it!" I exclaimed. "That's probably why I felt that the whole of time existed in those fleeting moments back in that meditation hall. Hmm ... so meditation is ultimately the bringing of time to an end. The word attentive is making more sense to me now. Basically, as long as I think there's time, I'm not in the present. This also clarifies your video-editor example, when you said that being in the present (aka attentive) allows you to dodge the knife (time) because there is no content (thinking) to chop up in that exact moment. There's quietness in being attentive which brings about a state of beingness. Whoa ... now I better understand the word be. To be is a state in which I know there's nowhere to go and no time to get there." I felt awed as neurons wired together in my head.

"Now you know why the first thing I asked you to do this morning, before we started this walk, was to listen without allowing your past experiences and knowledge to intervene," the voice responded. "You're always listening and seeing with what you know. Now you're learning to listen from a place of silence. A place that's not time bound. In that place of absolute silence, as you've experienced, you have no conclusions, you have no motives, you don't want anything. In that state you're fully and effortlessly attentive."

"Okay ... Now I also better understand why you said that to the 'genius within' all of time is here and now. The genius is not a thinker; the genius is simply, effortlessly attentive in every moment, making no room for thought. Hmm ... being fully attentive at every moment ... Why aren't I able to always be fully attentive in every moment?" I asked the voice, eager and excited to hear his answer.

The voice chuckled. "Well ... It takes a great amount of energy to be attentive and examine yourself."

"Where do I get that energy from?"

"You tell me. Where did that state of energy come from when you went on your Vipassana retreat?"

"I don't know. It just came," I replied.

"Let me rephrase my question: what did you do for those ten days?"

"Nothing. All I had to do was to meditate all day long."

"Did you have to think about buying food and preparing it? Or was it all just done for you? ... Did you have to think about cleaning? ... Did you have to speak and interact with others? ... Did you have any errands you needed to run? You see what I am getting at?

"This energy doesn't come from outside of you. This energy comes into being when you learn how to stop dissipating it," the voice continued. "When you learn how to take your hands off the steering wheel and stop resisting and trying to analyze and rationalize everything, that's when you stop dissipating energy. I know it's not very tangible for the logical mind just yet, but when you learn to be, then that energy naturally comes into being because its already there."

I sat down with this new information and enjoyed the fact that I fully understood what was being said to me. I felt a shift in my state of being. I wanted to learn more.

The voice returned saying, "I want to emphasize that the thinking is what creates content, and the content creation process is very much like breathing. Are you aware of every breath you took in today? You're constantly doing it all the time, but often automatically, reactively, with very little conscious attention as to how it impacts your experience, your video—aka reality.

"Hence the need to sharpen (quiet) the mind. The sharper (quieter) the mind is, the more conscious you become of your thoughts. When you consciously choose your thoughts, you can see how you form your experience by what you feel and what you think. If you don't like what you see, then look to your thoughts and choose thoughts that will support your true desires. I know ... easier said than done."

"There's no need to struggle to live in and try to control what you call the future," the voice continued. "Because just like that video, there is no future; you create it. If you want the video to continue the way you want it to, all you need to do is create new deliberate content for the video. Your next step is always right here, in this moment, within the timeline, to think of what content you'd like to add, and then create it. I'll say it again and again, it's a matter of sharpening the mind and being consciously aware of how you wish to approach your life. That's a nice way of saying, pull it together.

"So now you know that thought comes first and experience is always secondary. It's never the other way around. You'll never have the experience and then base the thought around it. Your experience is always a direct reflection of what you're thinking. Take a moment to consider this and sit with what I said."

Feeling overwhelmed, I said, "That's a lot to digest. Are you saying that my actual experience is a direct reflection of what I'm thinking? Or are you saying that my perception of my experience comes as a direct reflection of what I'm thinking?"

"We already covered the answer to both of those questions, but let's look at it together once more from a different angle. First, tell me, what do you mean by perception?" The voice asked.

"How I see something ...?" I responded hesitantly.

"Can you see that tree over there?" The voice asked.

I quickly responded "I do."

"Do you see the tree as it is? or do you see the tree through the glasses of your previous memories? Meaning are you using your existing knowledge to observe this tree? Or are you just looking at this tree with a quiet mind?" the voice asked.

For a moment I understood his question but then the screen was blurry again. I kept silent.

He continued, saying, "We've talked about perception, and previously we've talked about thought. But we haven't covered the word experience. Tell me, what does experience mean to you?" The voice asked.

"Hmm ... well ... the way I see it, is that when I am experiencing something, I am going through it. So, to me, experience is to go through something." I answered candidly.

"As you go through an experience, you accumulate knowledge ... Now, this knowledge, which is accumulated experience, gets stored up as memory, right?" the voice asked.

I nodded, saying, "I'm following."

"My question to you is, once again, can you look at this tree without the intervention of all the previous knowledge you have accumulated? In other words, can you look at this tree as a child who is observing this tree for the first time? as a child who has no motive, but completely filled with curiosity and is attentively observing this tree in awe and amazement."

After some moments of silence, I said, "I don't think it's possible to look at the tree through a child's eyes anymore. For me at least, it all happens so fast, when I look at the tree, I immediately 'know' it's a tree."

85

"What happens to your attention when you look at the tree and say 'I know' that this is a tree?" the voice asked.

"I don't really give it much attention because I already know it's a tree." I replied.

"So what you are saying is that you don't give it attention because you 'think' that you already know what it is from your existing 'content', aka knowledge that you have collected. That's why you 'think' that you cannot see it through a child's eyes. Because, tell me, what's the difference between you and a child?" the voice asked.

"The content," I responded contemplatively. And then it all clicked and I said "Ahh! I see ... just like that character in that video editor example, I'm continuously branching off my existing content." I then said, "And since we also established that when there's complete attention just like that surgeon, then it's possible to bring thought to an end. So if I'm not mistaken, what you're asking me is whether or not I'm capable of observing the tree with complete attention without having an idea of what I think it is. Meaning, there's no thought in the mix."

The voice came back saying, "Exactly. You've done it before, dear one ... Yet you still believe that you can't be fully attentive and see through a child's eyes.

"But for now, you are learning that to be able to fully perceive what's right in front of you, has to do with the clarity of your perception and whether or not it's distorted by your existing memory. If the latter was the case, then in that state of distortion, your perception has nothing to do with what you're looking at in the present moment.

"So now you can see that the word attention means direct perception. Seeing what is as it is. And that is exactly what happened that night back at university. Yes! The moment you surrendered and said you were going to do the best you could with whatever time you had was the moment when the genius came out. The genius had complete attention in the moment, and as such, did not allow thought to take over. By doing that, the genius was able to harness all of the energy that could've been dissipated by an occupied mind that is constantly thinking and worrying. Afraid of this and afraid of that. In that moment, you freed the mind of occupation.

"The mind was no longer a hostage to its self-created fear. It was able to harness all of that energy and use it to stay effortlessly attentive in the moment. Suddenly it was 7:30 am. Yes, that's also why the genius had no fear. The genius had a quiet and attentive mind. That's why I said earlier, you've done it before but still believe that you can't be fully attentive and see through a child's eyes.

"Now you can clearly see that fear is a result of time, thought and lack of attention ..." the voice said as he waited on me to respond.

"The moment you let go of the worry of not having enough time and intended to do the best you could with whatever time you had left. In that exact moment, the mind stopped worrying, time came to an end, thought came to an end and fear also came to an end. This interval between what is now and what will be in the future was gone. No more stressing and dissipating energy, but simply doing," the voice firmly stated.

"Ha! That's true ..." I responded in awe. I continued to say, "Fear ... it was non-existent in that state of mind. It's also true that I had no sense of time and my mind was not occupied with thought. It was completely present with the work at hand."

"We've been over it a hundred times now ... but going back to that video editor example ... tell me who created that video? It was you, wasn't it?" the voice asked.

"Yes," I replied.

"You created your invention, which is this video, and then later you watched yourself in the video. So you're the character in the video, you're the person who created the video and you're also the person who is watching and editing the video. It's all you. My next question to you is ... the video itself where did it come from?" the voice asked.

"I thought of it," I quickly replied.

"Did you hear what you just said? You essentially said that the video came from a thought that you had that said, 'I'm going to create the video.' So again, you are the creator of the video, the actual content of the video and the observer of the video; all of which came from a thought. Thought gave birth to that entire experience. Does this answer your previous questions?" the voice asked, wanting to make sure I was following along.

The clarity that comes forth from this voice ... when he speaks, I see clearly, but when he's gone, it's all blurry again.

He then said, "So again, at the base, it's thought that creates. A thought creates a cause which has an effect that turns into a cause, and it continues, giving birth to an experience. I'll explain this cause and effect cycle later on today. But for now, after many experiences, you end up having a bank of thoughts and beliefs–aka content–from which you operate. If we go even further back to basics, the outer world that you perceive depends solely on your internal vibrational frequency," the voice said, speaking calmly, yet firmly.

"Wait a minute," I said. "You first said that it's thought that ultimately creates. Then you said that the outer-perceived world depends on my internal vibrational frequency. Do my thoughts affect my vibrational frequency?"

"Absolutely, dear one. Like I said before, if there is only one thing you'd take away from our conversation today. It would be that your thoughts formulate your world. No matter what situation you find yourself experiencing or going through–whether it's comfortable or not–know that it's there to teach you something new. It's there to help you grow and set you up for what is yet to come," the voice said cheerfully.

"Okay. That makes sense," I said. "But what about victims of abuse? Did they create the other person who inflicted harm on them?"

"Look to your right," the voice replied in a soft compassionate tone. "You see that bee over there? Tell me, did the bee create the flower?"

"Is this a trick question?" I asked.

The voice chortled and said, "Being skeptical is good, but keep it on a healthy leash. Otherwise you might block information that could serve you, from coming to you ... You see. As a human being existing in this dimension, there may be times when the universe needs to shock you out of your complacency. Out of your apathy. Sometimes it's the only way that you learn. These shocks can come in uncomfortable forms. Death of a relative, an accident, a natural disaster and other scenarios. These shocks literally jolt you into other realities of being.

"If you let go of judgment and of being attached to what happened to you. It gets easier not to project and blame others for what has happened to you. Soon, you will learn, that the person who inflicted harm to you is also a portion of you. I lost you with that one, but it'll become clearer later in our conversation.

"Going back to your initial question, challenges and situations will arise. They're there. Just like the bee, the flower and the sun. They're all just there. You didn't create them. However, in every moment you have the power to consciously act, to create, regardless of the influences that surround you and regardless of what situation you find yourself in. In that moment when the challenge presents itself, if you create thoughts that allow you to believe that you can stabilize this threat, then that's what you'll create. First, you want to quiet the mind. Because when you are in a threatening situation, generally you feel you don't have time to think. When you slow down, with a quiet mind, you'll be capable of creating a favorable scenario. Remember, conscious creation comes from quietness.

"Did the gazelle create the lion? Does the gazelle sit down and blame the lion for going after it and wanting to eat it? Or does the gazelle participate in the experience and learn from it? Whenever you get an experience, learn to participate within your experience. Learn to be a full participant within your physical body. Learn how to simultaneously observe your experience, its impact and the effect it has on you. You always get results from all of your experiences. The universe does not give you an experience because it's bored. There is always something to learn."

After a pause, he added, "It's a game of frequency. The universe doesn't see right or wrong, good or bad. From the universe's eye, you are energy vibrating at a frequency. What frequency bracket do you operate in? That's the question. Only frequencies within that bracket affect you. Everything is connected vibrationally. Everything that you live is what you believe. If you have a low vibration or frequency, then everything that comes to you is a low vibration. Some vibrate so low that they need an experience with the same level of frequency to knock them out of the low-frequency bracket and into a higher one. Yes, just like a slingshot. The universe would pull you back to give you enough momentum to catapult you into another frequency bracket.

Hesitantly, I asked, "What about tragedies and disasters where thousands of people are affected? I'm having a hard time understanding what happened to those people. They didn't even have a chance to participate in their experience. How are they not victims?"

The voice replied in a neutral tone: "Every life upon the surface of the earth is sacred. Those individuals who died from a volcano erupting are not victims. Victims to who exactly? Victims of a higher power? Victims of Earth?

"What happened to your family when your grandfather died? Things changed. Didn't they? The family members came closer to one another, more than ever before. Right? Although only one soul left its body behind, this soul affected many. You understand what I'm saying? The individuals who died from a natural disaster or similar scenario played a role in the evolution of many. What happens

90

to them affects the consciousness of not only the Earth but also of all the people involved. They bring about a shift in consciousness, because they'll leave a psychic impact on the rest. Just like the effect your grandfather had on your family. Remember ... everything is integrated together; you are not a separate individual."

The voice then said, "I want you to understand that it's not necessarily about what's happening to you or the situation in which you find yourself. It is the thoughts that you create while you're participating in the experience. The truth, in its purest and virgin form, is that you create your reality. What you're yearning for is to learn how to connect what you think with how you feel so you can better navigate this world of frequency.

"To be able to navigate this world of frequency, you want to monitor and watch your thoughts. That's why it is important to get to know the self. Know thyself; you get it now? Clarity and recognition of your own power are the bottom line. Your thoughts form your world, and because you're kept from being an independent thinker, you fluctuate, and end up creating more of what others want you to think you can or cannot create.

"Yes, that's how you end up living someone else's life and yet truly believe and think you're living a life of your own. You want to make it your intention to stay very clear, to stay centered and to always bring yourself into the moment. Stop living in the future or living in the past. Live right now.

"Ask yourself what you want, so you can begin to attract more of it to you. I know the latter wasn't tangible enough for the logical mind. Again, let me clarify. Remember that bee we saw earlier? A flower needs to be pollinated. To encourage bees to visit it, the flower develops colourful petals and an attractive scent. In other words, the flower broadcasts a certain frequency that will attract the bees. That flower is you and that bee is what you are wanting to attract. Learn from the flowers. You are in nature for a reason."

Liking the concept, I asked, "How do I do like the flower? How do I broadcast a frequency that will attract what I want?"

"Think of your mind as a radio," the voice replied. "Because it really is. Every time you throw a thought out there, that thought broadcasts a signal, a frequency, that says, 'Oh hey there, everyone and everything in the universe who's listening to this radio station—to this frequency I'm broadcasting—you're welcome to come shape my reality.' So now what happens? All those vibrational frequencies who are tuned into that frequency range can now hear you and, better yet, see you. It's a matter of learning how to tune your frequency to attract only experiences that you like. In this case, to attract bees and not anything else that doesn't serve you.

"Oh!" I felt my enthusiasm rise even more. "Is this why you keep jabbering about taming the mind and consciously creating thoughts?"

"Yes. That's why I keep reminding you to monitor and be mindful of your thoughts. But thanks for the compliment. Remember, the universe thinks in terms of vibrational frequency. From the universe's perspective, there is no good or bad. There is simply a vibrational frequency, and you are the one who is responsible for your own vibrational frequency. You are the content creator. By taking conscious responsibility for your thoughts, you'll no longer attract or broadcast a frequency you don't wish to attract."

"You're saying that this is a game of frequency?" I asked.

"Yes, it's a magnetic force that attracts things of a like frequency. You're learning how to shift your frequency, so that you can change your reality. First, you want to shift the mind before you can shift your reality. To be able to shift the mind, you want to tame it. That's what you're doing with Vipassana meditation, breathing and yoga.

"You're continuously creating your reality even if you don't know you're doing it. You've been doing this your entire life. Remember what I told you this morning? I told you that I can't predict the

92

future for you. Now, knowing what you've learned thus far, you can put the pieces of the puzzle together and realize that you don't need me to predict the future for you. Why? Because you're beginning to really understand how the future works.

"See, I'm here simply to guide you, so you can trust yourself enough to say, 'You know what, even though this new path scares me, because it's all new and uncertain, I know with every single fiber of my being, that it's the right thing to do.' Does that make sense to you? Because when you get to that point, and you will–trust me, it's a process that many go through–you'll have far less anxiety and headaches about the choices you think you should or you shouldn't do. Because with this new way of being, you're learning to go with the flow and not resist your inner guidance–remember the horse. Having less resistance means having less suffering, meaning you're on track."

CHAPTER 13

LETTING GO

The voice's mention of being on track brought me back to the track on which I stood. I continued on along it, enjoying the solitude and lush jungle surrounding me. I could hear the birds still singing as the sunrays made their way through the jungle. Insects were everywhere, but they no longer bothered me, although bites covered my feet and legs.

Before I'd gone very far, the voice continued, "So now you can clearly see that letting go is an act of freedom in and of itself. Because when you let go, you allow help to come in. It's scariest and is most uncomfortable in the beginning. Just like that bungee jump or that sky dive, you build up a lot of fear just before the jump only to realize later on that it wasn't necessary after all. Truth is, in time, you'll conclude from your own life experience that you're being supported by an invisible cushion that you can't necessarily see, but you can absolutely feel its presence with you.

"It's truly a freeing experience. It's what that horse felt when you were finally able to gain its trust. The moment that horse trusted you, let go and surrendered, it immediately started to see and enjoy the bliss that has always been there, yet was fogged by its own mind. So now you can see clearly that by allowing the mind to take the backseat, you begin to allow help to come through. It's like having a close friend, who you love dearly and know is need of help, but when you reach out and offer them your support, they turn it down because they're stuck in their head.

"They're not consciously aware of it, but they choose not to allow help to come in, because they're wanting to preserve the reputation of whatever image they've built of themselves, in their own heads, to themselves. Hence, they choose to go through pain or suffering whichever word you want to choose. This is what I meant when we talked about the need to be in a state of receptivity earlier this morning—not so different from your Vipassana experience, either. As soon as you got yourself in a receptive state after that shaky first day, the entire experience was transformational, wasn't it?

I interrupted the voice, saying, "I'm connecting the dots together. When you tied the concept of receptivity back to my Vipassana experience, I realized that being in a receptive state is essentially what we've discussed earlier; it's to let go of any expectations from my experience ... and as I do that, I indirectly let go of distortion, and I give myself the freedom to perceive what is. That's when I receive insight. Fascinating! I think I just understood the word insight."

After a pause, I added, "Insight is direct perception of what is, without the involvement of memory!"

"Brilliant!" the voice said, full of excitement. "So you see this invisible cushion that's always available and wanting to support you can't support you unless you allow it to. Be willing to receive what's being sent your way. To get to that state of receptivity, as you already know, you want to get out of your head.

"To be very clear, the act of letting go doesn't mean you become a potato. It means being fully engaged in life while allowing help and guidance to come through. Again, you've experienced this, and you know what happens when you let go of control and allow the genius dude inside to do his thing. You don't need to know the how or the why. Simply be fully engaged with life and take action from a place of guidance and inner knowing. You'll find that although there'll be times where the path might seem treacherous, you know deep inside you that you're never alone."

I interrupted the voice saying, "Question: Is it possible to be in a state of surrender and receptivity all the time?" As I said that, it was the first time that I became fully conscious of the fact that I was truly having a conversation with a 'voice.' My mind immediately jumped on that opportunity, and my thoughts began to race back and forth, and, of course, more questions bubbled up.

Luckily, the voice came back and interrupted my train of thoughts by saying, "We've already answered that question. You only ask me such questions because you're identifying with your thoughts right now." And then he disappeared again.

I didn't understand what he meant by that sentence, but I continued to walk around exploring the jungle. That was when I ran across a funny looking tree that had its roots above ground, as if it stood on many spindly legs. I stood by this tree staring at its roots, baffled at how they grew like that.

The voice crept up on me, saying, "Have you noticed that everything we've talked about today all boils down to freedom, a different kind of freedom to what you've been accustomed? It's the internal kind of freedom, the kind you're seeking but don't know it. It's the freedom from expectations, the freedom from anything that's going to limit you, define you and suppress any of your natural abilities. You're not the only one seeking this. When I asked you earlier what it was you were looking for, what I heard you say to me is I want to be me. So if you're wanting to be you, then to be able to be you, you'll need to understand what is you, right? Otherwise, how can you be you?

"So here you are, right now, at a point where you're ready

to be you, and you want to be you, but you're stuck. Why? Because before you can get this freedom you're seeking, you need to find out what you are. And indirectly, who you truly are.

"To find out who you truly are, you want to experience the moment. Remember, experience means to go through something. In this case to go through the moment. My question to you is, do you ever fully go through the entire moment?" The voice paused before continuing, "Don't go searching for an answer. It's not about the answer, remember? It's about the state of mind with which you look at the question.

"See ... as long as you're caught up in your thoughts, you are not fully present in the moment, and as such, you're not able to receive the information that's being shown to you in the mirror. Meaning you're not actually going through the moment. You're not experiencing the moment. Therefore, you're missing the insight you're seeking. The trick is to have that knowing always in your moments, because who you are comes out of that moment.

"How do I put this differently? I want you to imagine yourself looking at a mirror, any mirror, it doesn't matter. Now stare in the mirror. What is this mirror doing for you? It's reflecting back to you all that is.

"Each of your individual experiences are unique for you; and what you need to experience is being reflected back to you right here, right now, in this moment. If you're caught up in your thoughts and not fully present, it's like having a massive mirror right in front your face that's reflecting back to you all you seek, but you're not looking at it and in it. Why? You guessed it ... because you're looking in your head all the time. And because you're in your head most of the time, you can't see you. You then tell yourself, 'I don't have the answers to the questions I seek,' and you come to me asking me questions like, 'Is it possible to be in a state of surrender and receptivity all the time?' Or 'Who am I?'

"To find out what you are, it would be simpler for you to identify with what you are not. As you observe your thoughts, simply recognize that these thoughts are appearing and disappearing. But here's the twist: there is something which perceives the thoughts. It has no name, no shape, no form, no size. It just is. It doesn't need anything. It doesn't want anything. It's always there, and it doesn't change. It simply observes the thoughts. Therefore, you are not your thoughts. Although most times you identify as them.

"But you already know the latter from your meditation practice. Now, similar to your thoughts, the body comes and goes. There is something which perceives the body which doesn't change. Therefore, you are not the body. If it's hard for you to accept the latter, just imagine, for example, that you lost a limb; you're still you, aren't you? There you go.

"Now each time you recognize something that you are not, it's like taking off a layer of your clothing, and when you're standing there naked, what remains is what you are."

I grinned with excitement and interrupted the voice, yelling, "The perceiver! Whoa! You couldn't have started with that example from the beginning? You really had to dance around it and philosophize before you could put it in simple terms?"

I got chills and goosebumps all over my body. We'd talked about the concept of the perceiver and the observer earlier, but that was the first time I'd felt it in my body. That was when I truly accepted that registering something merely at an intellectual level is not enough to fully understand what's being said. I want to feel or experience what's being said to me to fully understand it.

I began to better understand what my Vipassana practice was teaching me. Vipassana taught me to take away the mental interpretation and the label of the experience and simply meet sensations as they are, as they arise, without trying to change them, get rid of them, become them, or even expect anything from my experience at any moment. And as I do that, I experience the observer. The observer knows that all that exists is in the present moment. Whoa ... It does take the intellect some time to catch up, I thought. This path, this journey, continued to humble me again and again.

In that moment, my body felt as if it had been struck by lightning. I stopped walking, looked around me and found a log from a broken tree to sit on. I sat there in silence, watching some massive ants walk up my feet and legs.

"Does letting go make more sense to you now?" the voice asked eventually. "You want to allow yourself to be guided, and to do so, you want to develop trust in yourself, develop that relationship with the dude inside." The voice faded away again.

Minutes passed in silence, and then I decided to continue walking.

The voice popped up again saying, "You still don't trust yourself and that's normal because your current belief is rooted in the mentality of lack, the mentality of not enough. When you're rooted in that mentality–which, unfortunately, a lot of people are–it constructs your entire belief system.

"Since you create based on what you believe, not consciously, but otherwise. You'll keep banging your head against the wall, feeling and believing that you can't and now you actually can't. Why? Because you'll be proving yourself right every single time. Your mind is saying, I know I can't and hence I can't. Period. Your mind is happy and comfortable knowing that it's right, because that means it knows the answer. That makes it feel, wait for it ... yes, you're right ... safe!

"Can't you hear them? They whisper ... they're laughing and saying, 'If he only knew who walks next to him every step of the way.' All you need to do is keep moving forward and trust that you're safe. I'm very excited for what's to come for you. You're in the midst of rediscovering your freedom and transforming your reality from a place of fear and chaos into a place of freedom. Simply because you intend it and you know that you can do it.

"As you continue to look at your beliefs and notice where there's cracks, you begin to change the way you view yourself and, consequently, the way you view the world. Then, all of a sudden, all these different doors will open to you, because now you can see them. Why? Because you slowed down and grabbed your mind by the balls. With this new way of being, you are the one who's in control. You are the one who's guiding this vehicle, and your mind will take the backseat.

"This was the first thing I brought up to you earlier this morning. The whole process is a slightly uncomfortable dance. You see it now? It's not about trying to get there as if it's a destination, as if what you're looking for is something outside of you, and when you get there you're done. That perception can't be further from the truth. Freedom is not a destination. When you think it's a destination, you're still stuck in limitation because that 'destination' is a boundary in and of itself.

Freedom always has somewhere else to go. When you find yourself saying you're free, you're furthest from being free, because freedom knows no bounds. Free means there's always more to go. In other words, if you think you're free now, you can still be freer. And if you tell yourself, 'Ahh, okay, now I'm free.' Remember, you can still be freer! That's the flight into freedom. It's boundless.

"Remember that time when you were walking down the street and ran into a young lady whose dog jumped on you? She got nervous, but you calmed her down when you told her you loved dogs. One thing led to another and you ended up telling her you'd been wanting to get a dog, but you didn't want to keep it in an apartment. Remember what she said? She said, 'Look at my dog; he's very happy. He has no clue that he can have more space.' Is the fog slightly clearing up now with this new way of looking at what freedom is? When you say you're free you simply don't know that you can have more of it."

CHAPTER 14

ALLOW INFORMATION TO COME TO YOU

The voice continued, "I can hear them say, 'The dude can do whatever he wants,' and then they whisper, 'He simply forgot his strength.' Yes, that's you; you forgot your strength, and that's why you doubt and question yourself. That's the main reason behind why you need data. You want and look for proof before you can accept anything outside of the shoebox you've been put in.

"I want you to visualize this shoebox with me. Now, place yourself in the center of it. Look around you and notice the walls that surround you. These walls and ceiling define the boundaries of information that you perceive to be legitimate. Meaning, everything you understand and everything that makes sense to you is within these walls. They define your perceptions, your experiences and really these walls define your world–or, at least, what you currently perceive to be your world. Again, it's your shoebox. So this world of yours can be as simple or as complex as you design it to be. It's your world, after all.

"What's happening at this time is that you have large amounts of information finding its way to you. This new information isn't necessarily coming in the format you've been accustomed to while

103

living within your box. Yes, we're dealing with a compatibly issue here. This incoming information is expansive. It has a different format to what your 'operating system' aka 'belief system' is used to. As such, it might be perceived as contradictory and controversial to what you already know, or what you think you know.

"The latter makes it hard for you to get out of your shoebox and accept all this new information that's coming in from different directions and in large quantities, varieties and formats. This is making you overwhelmed, confused and wanting to seek more data and proof before you can allow yourself to get out of the box. As such, what ends up happening? You end up going nowhere. Why? Because you're only allowing certain information to come in, in certain and specific ways. I totally get it.

"What I want you to know is that you don't need to get yourself out of the box you find yourself in if that's too much at the moment. You can begin by expanding the existing one. This box of yours is alive, and it's dynamic. The box will expand with you. Remember, this box is you. The walls of this shoebox are the outline of who you are. Because, after all, who you are is a whole bunch of perceptions. With this approach, your challenge will be with the integration of the new information with the old. Why would that be a challenge? Because like I mentioned earlier, this new information might be perceived as controversial to your logical mind right now. If you find yourself at that point, add something to your life that will act as a catalyst to help you integrate this information and initiate your expansion.

"Keep in mind that when you're in growth mode, you're working towards allowing information to come in. When you allow information to enter, in whatever way it wants, you begin to expand the region of the shoebox in which you live. The shoebox defines the boundaries of information you presently deem legitimate, which might have changed from what you might have thought was legitimate a minute ago.

"You see? This box is constantly changing. And what makes the expansion of this shoebox even harder? Your need to have your ducks in a row, so to speak. You like to keep your life and all of your 'data' organized. But here's the thing: when you're attempting to become a greater being, all that data will need to be reshuffled, re-analyzed and compared to a new line of code. That data will need to be compared to a new program, a new operating system, a new belief system.

"It's, quite literally, as if you're reformatting your computer and installing a new operating system. It's going to be temporarily disruptive. And yes, a scrambling of data will need to take place. That's why, at times, you might think you're going crazy and feel you can't differentiate between what's real and what's not. Now you know the answer to the question you asked me yesterday whilst in your medi-ation. No, dear one, you're not going crazy. In fact, whenever you feel that way, rejoice, because in plain English you're being upgraded.

"Nevertheless, I completely understand why you want and seek proof, and to be very clear, there's nothing wrong with that. It's just that when outside proof is the only way for you to source your answers, you'll always be running in circles–and I don't want to see you run in circles."

CHAPTER 15

A NEW CYCLE

He then said, "This phase is preparing you to start a new cycle and move into a different dimension of being. From one who's a thinker into one who's a perceiver—a feeler. As such, certain leadership qualities are being called out, because it's time for you to practice being a leader. A leader of your own life story. What does a good leader do? He trusts his skills. Remember this: power in and of itself is dormant. It means nothing. It's how you use that power that yields results. And you, my friend, have been using your power in a way that ultimately hurts you. Because you think it's safe. You see the irony in that?

"What else does a leader want to do? We've established that he wants to develop trust in himself first and foremost, right? Although there'll be times when you'll want confirmation, if you always look outside of you for that, life will be much harder than it needs to be. Again, when you're being guided by your gut, by your intuition, and by all your other faculties, and not favoring one over the other—sometimes it's more difficult than other times—then there's no such thing as having a right or wrong experience. Why? Because each and every experience offers you a valuable way to learn about yourself, which at the end of the day yields strength.

"When you look at it this way, all of a sudden there's a whole lot less pressure on your shoulders, isn't there? You've just learned that it's how you see things that makes the difference. It's not what you see. All we did right there was change your perception, and your reality changed along with it. That's why I was teasing you earlier on and told you that you've voluntarily put all this pressure on your shoulders. It's just a matter of changing your perception."

I looked to my left and I saw another funky tree similar to the one I'd seen before, but this one was even more interesting. Many roots forked out of one trunk and many other roots branched out of each one of those roots, all before they even met the ground. Now that's something I hadn't seen before.

"Speaking of perception," the voice said, "I still haven't addressed the concept of failure with you. Tell me, what is failure to you? Would you say you're failing in life right now? If so, what precisely are you failing at? I sense that at a subconscious level your definition of failure and success is somehow tied to money. However, for you, the issue is not with the making of money. It's worse. The issue is that money, because you translate it into security, overrides your emotional contentment. That's where I get all choked up right now, because it limits my ability, which is your ability, to express my own individuality.

"What I am saying, is that once again, you have been accustomed to prefer to do things that will keep you safe. That way of living is preventing you from expressing your own individuality, which is what you're here to experience in the first place. No, there's nothing wrong with that. Wrong is simply your perception of it. The real question is ... does it feel good to you? What may have felt good to you a moment ago, with this new realization, might no longer feel that way. Which means that you're ready for something different, and that something different is a shift of consciousness, which is followed by fear, the fear of not knowing what's coming.

"You're in an interesting process right now. You're pulling a lobster. Yes, you heard me right, I said you're pulling a lobster. Lobsters molt to grow. They shed their entire outer shell, and then they eat the shell to retain the nutrients and speed up the hardening of their new shell. Until the new shell hardens around their body, they go into hiding. In a way, you're in your own molting process. You're on a path of transformation and becoming. You're considering your current life structures, and–although structure provides safety and stability as you move and grow in the world–on this path you're on right now, you're wanting to break free from the current form in order to grow into a higher way.

"Just like the lobster does each time it sheds its shell and eats it, it's about you harvesting the lessons of your past experiences in order to evolve and grow into a form that will fully honor who you're now becoming. This process of expanding your perception of the possible, and challenging yourself to see beyond what you and others may have thought to be possible yesterday, can be perceived as an uphill battle or a hard time in your life. But I want you to see it for what it is, and that is that you're creating a whole new form/structure that honors your natural gifts, and honors who you truly came here to be. It's beautiful. It's poetic.

"What that means is that there are aspects of you and of your life that will need to perish. You've used them for what they were intended for. You've learned all the lessons you were supposed to learn from them to enable you to walk in your truth and give you the skills needed to do what you're meant to do here in this lifetime. You're becoming more of an independent thinker versus one whose ideas are based on concepts that were made for him. This is how you realize who you really are.

109

"Earlier, we talked about what freedom meant to you. At this stage of our interaction, we can also add to that definition. Freedom also means being an independent thinker. Now there's nothing that says you can't be an independent thinker. It's only you believing that you can't, that you don't know whether you should or shouldn't or if it's going to be a disaster, a failure or all of the above that stops you. Which, again, takes us back to fear. Yes, there's a lot of fear haunting humanity.

"You're simply someone who's ready to make new choices, and you're afraid because you don't know what your choices are going to look like at the end of the day. You and many others have the tendency to interpret fear as a sign that something's going to go wrong, so rather than pursuing what's on your mind, you remain where you are because it's safe. But where is your curiosity in all of this? Where is your livelihood in all of this? Have you lost your curiosity about life in favor of being safe? Or do you allow your curiosity to still be active while being mindful of what's in front of you? For some reason, you seem to think that you can only have one or the other, curiosity or safety. I'm telling you that you can have both. You can have anything you want. Take my word for it: curiosity didn't kill that cat.

"To tie up the failure component piece before I forget. If this so-called failure is real to you, then ask yourself, who is it that considers what you're doing in your life a failure? Is it according to you? Is it according to your parents? Society? Friends? Who is it? What you'll come to realize is that it boils down to the fact that others' validation of you is of most importance to you. In other words, you're creating your own limitations by allowing yourself to only live under the influences, the frequencies, that've been imposed upon you.

"Because it's so subtle and has become a part of your belief system, it's a habit now, even though it might not feel like that's the case. It's a pattern of behavior that you're not necessarily aware of. At the same time, an urge has been awakened within you, one that, all

110

of sudden, is nudging you to pursue a purposeful life, a life of service. But you have no clue what you're supposed to be doing and whether or not you can actually do it.

CHAPTER 16

ETERNAL IDENTITY

The voice's accuracy mesmerized me. I didn't want him to stop. With a whole lot of curiosity, I asked, "What triggered this urge for a new cycle? And why now?"

The voice replied with a smile in his tone, "At this point in your life, you've become more in touch with who you truly are; in other words, your soul, your eternal identity. Your eternal identity does not change with the different phases (video cuts) of your life. As you continue to tame your mind and learn more about your inner being, you become aware of your urges, which is what's happening to you right now. That's what triggers this urge of yours. Soon you'll start to cooperate more with your soul's desires, and the louder and the clearer you can hear your true self, the more you'll learn and remember about who you truly are.

"I can feel your resistance to this concept of eternal identity. This is similar to that compatibility issue where the format of the information can't be processed.

"The issue isn't with the information. The main issue is with the format of the information. I'll change the format. Here's how you

113

can think of it. You used to play video games. Remember how you were able to position characters, the players, at different locations on the map before the game started? You chose where the character would spawn, right?"

"Yeah, I did actually. Gosh, I miss playing those games!" I responded cheerfully.

"Okay. Now, visualize yourself back in that room playing that video game. Visualize yourself choosing a character that will have the right skills, the natural abilities, to help you accomplish what you want to achieve in the game. After choosing the character, the avatar, you then have the option to spawn at a specific location or culture medium in the game. You chose your spawning location based on where the need was.

"Every time the character in the game died, it either respawned in the same location or you, the player, had the option to change the spawning location of the character. Notice that you're the one watching the screen and playing the game. Tell me ... when the character died in the game, did you, the player, die with the character?"

I shook my head. "Of course not."

"Now you can see that you don't die, dear one. You're simply controlling the character with your joystick. Remember? You are the perceiver of the game. Where it gets tricky is when you get attached to the character in the game and get emotionally invested. When that happens, you begin to think you are the character in the game. I can feel your entire body resonating with this. Now you're truly understanding what we've been talking about all day, from the concept of choosing your family, your culture medium, to the concept of detachment, to the concept of being the creator, to the concept of tapping into the genius who's simply perceiving it all. Now you can see why you're wanting to tame the mind, because as soon as you quiet the mind, you begin to see with unprecedented clarity where the character begins and ends and where you begin and don't end.

Yes, you are a continuous being.

"Now you know who's talking to you. Now you know who I am and who you are. Again, and again. I'm always with you. I want you to understand that you came here with natural abilities that are needed on your planet earth. That's why I started off this conversation today by saying that you came here to express a unique life force that can only be translated through you, through your vehicle. Now you can also understand why I used the metaphor of unclogging the pipes. With the pipes unclogged, you can allow this life force—something that is much bigger than you—to come through the pipes, so to speak.

"When you overcome your fear of belonging, of acceptance and of fitting in, and then allow yourself to be who you are and who you came here to be, you don't just serve you, you also serve the world you occupy. So now if you look at it for what it is, you can see what I meant by eternal identity. In this game, this mind game, when you respawn as the character, you temporarily lose memory of you and you identify with the character.

"Now how you choose to express your individuality is entirely up to you. That was simply a message for you to embrace what makes you different, and to express the wholeness of your True Self. Being authentic and true to yourself is the greatest gift you can give to the world and to yourself. Be uniquely you.

"Your biggest obstacle right now is that you feel that if you choose your own desires based on your inner truth, those who mean a lot to you will reject you. Yes, that's how it is for you. So, essentially, you have this fear of being abandoned for being you. For now, look at it from a logical point of view. What you're essentially telling yourself is, 'I need to adhere to society or else.' Tell me ... where's the time for relaxation when you're always trying to fit in, when you're always trying to prove yourself to somebody?"

"I'm never relaxed," I replied. "I always have stuff on my mind."

The voice laughed and said, "I feel and understand what

115

you're going through. They're asking me to say this to you: remind him once again that he simply forgot his strength, and that doesn't mean he doesn't have it. You just momentarily forgot your strength. Why? Because you're not used to using it. And you know what they say: if you don't use it, you lose it. What I mean by this is that no one has power over you, yet you've given all your power to all of them. Does it make sense to you to give all of your power to others? Do you enjoy doing it? You don't, right? Then why do you continue doing it?

"Again, this isn't about you doing something the right way or the wrong way–we've been over that already. Obviously, you have your morals. This is about accepting things as they are, without outside influence and judgment. It's about you realizing that you have certain needs that you wish to fulfill, and those needs may not align with others who mean a lot to you. Your predicament is do I continue to choose to be this person in order to be accepted or do I choose to be me and see what happens?

"I'll tell you one thing for sure, when you continue to do things because you need acceptance, you'll always have a sense of something deep within that's missing in your life. And that's where you're at right now. That's why I'm here with you right now. So this is about you committing to you. But first, you want to know who you are, who you truly are. What do you like? What do you want? What are your desires? What would you like to try that you haven't tried before? What are your dreams? Do you even dare to dream? Do you dare to dream big? What excites you? What is your inner child wanting to play with next?

"You see what I'm saying? That's not the you that you project every day. The you that you needed to be up until this point was very structured. Why? Because it gave you safety and security. Many do it to a certain extent. However, you've put yourself in a box for far too long, and now you can feel that something is missing. You feel something's missing because most of your desires are fulfilled by

116

logical reasons such as safety, security and data. You feel that you must have something in order to feel something. But the reality is this; the feeling is already deep inside you. The feeling comes first and then the actual manifestation of that feeling follows. Not the other way around.

"You just have to feel what it is that you want within you, and then allow the Universe or God, which ever term feels more right to you, to bring experiences to you by bringing ideas, people and situations that are equal to the vibration of your emotion. Just like broadcasting a radio station frequency and attracting those who are listening to that frequency, as we talked about before. Now you have another answer to another question you had before I approached you. Now you know how you ended up here in the jungle. When you were sitting outside that building at the conference, and you visualized the jungle, and then made an intention from the deepest portion of your heart that you wanted to be here–although you had no clue how, where and when–and here you are. Your heart–not the physical heart, I'm talking about the energetic heart. The energy vortex, the chakra–is the steering wheel.

"The more you begin to live in alignment with who you really are, the more powerful your magnetic field gets and you begin to pull it all in like a magnet. Yes, you become a magnet to abundance. Why? Because you begin to live your life with such an inner knowing that your thoughts create your world, and you've become quite certain with such casualness that if you think of something, then it is. This is the theme I want to present to you over and over again whenever I get the opportunity. One of these days, you'll get it. Once you get it and begin to live it, you'll begin to change your life by aligning your thoughts with your true desires, and, as such, magnetizing more of it to you. It's not different from that time back in high school when you were taught how to magnetize a piece of metal. After those positively and negatively charged particles lined up within the metal, that piece of metal became a magnet.

"Ask yourself, what do you tend to favor in your life over anything else? What are your polarities? Do you see things as black and white? What rules do you live by? And until you know these things, you won't truly know who you really are, because who you are is based on your subconscious perception of you, which is based and rooted in your childhood and your early life—a time where you were not necessarily fully aware of what you were told and taught. You just absorbed it all like a sponge as if it was your truth. And since you're a very logical person, and you also want to see things very clearly, this is a great way for you to now clearly see you.

"You already know what I am about to tell you at a logical level, but when you don't pay attention to it, you end up hurting yourself. The words that you speak to yourself solidify your experience. So when you continually talk shit to yourself, shit that you're not even aware of, you're actually hurting yourself. Next time you look at the world and you say to yourself, 'I have to do this,' I want you to remember this: you don't 'have to' do anything. The reason why I'm saying this to you is because when you always tell yourself that you 'have to' do this or 'have to' do that, you're giving your power to something outside of you. You're limiting yourself, and you already told me that you don't want that.

"It's not going to be easy, but keep reminding yourself to come back to your center and keep reminding yourself that this life is a life that is meant to be lived by you. It's time to recognize your own strengths and weaknesses. No, not for the purpose of right or wrong, but for the purpose of understanding one and the other. Why? Because when you see both, you can see a clearer picture of the truth. With this clearer picture, when you begin to think that you're failing, you'll come to understand that there's no such thing as failure. It's just another perception that keeps you stuck in your place to show yourself that you're afraid to move.

"Failure is just another one of your labels that you love so much. You take this label and turn it into a belief because you put power into it, and then label it as failure. If you could learn to trust that there is no failure and that there's only stepping stones leading to whatever lessons you need to learn, you'll stop labeling things as failure and dwelling upon failure and begin to live.

"You'll begin to understand that what you think of yourself is of most importance. How you feel about yourself and what's important to you, versus how others feel about you, is of most importance. That doesn't mean that you don't want/need people to say nice things to you. No, but this is about living a life based on your truth, a life based on your own approval of you, versus a life based on other people's approval of you. Now that's independence. You're still far too emotionally attached to what other people think about you, the character, and if you're a leader in that position, guess what would happen? Not much. Because you'd not be able to stand still in your position.

"They're asking me to share this metaphor with you: they're saying, 'Ask him to attach his wings.' You have wings, but you just put them away. As a result of you having put them away, you believe that you don't have them, and therefore you can't fly. It's not that they're not there; it's just that you momentarily forgot about them. Your wings are your strength. That's what carries you, your strength. You decide ... do you want to focus on your strengths or on your weaknesses? Remember that weakness and strength are on the same trajectory. They're just on opposite sides. As a matter of fact, your perceived weakness when understood can become your greatest strength. Now with that in mind, look to yourself and see how you judge yourself and what limitations you so innocently place around yourself and hold onto, like a child holds on to their little dollies."

CHAPTER 17

EXPAND YOUR SHOEBOX—YOUR WORLD WILL EXPAND WITH IT

I didn't stop walking, though, at that point, I was getting worried about finding my way back because I felt I'd gone too far into the jungle. As soon as my thoughts attempted to overpower me, the voice chimed in again:

"You need to surrender. No, I'm not talking about surrendering to those thoughts that you just had. I'm talking about surrendering to what you know is truly for you. I'm talking about battling your ego. Again, ego is not a bad thing. We've been over that. In a way, ego tells you who you are, but who you are is basically a whole bunch of perceptions.

"Now, with you becoming more open, calmer and in touch with your true self, your ego is feeling out of place. Your ego, character, is scared and is saying, 'Wait a minute ... wait a minute ... something is happening right now, and I don't understand it. Holy moly, I'm losing control ... I need to be in control!' Yes, just like that horse.

"That's what's causing the constant discomfort you've been experiencing. Discomfort exists within the body when one refuses

121

the growth that the soul–the dude inside–needs to experience. This discomfort is telling you that you're obstructing your own growth. Remember that lobster? Imagine that lobster trying to grow, and it's pushing against its shell, but the shell isn't budging; it's resisting and trying to prevent the lobster from shedding it–letting it go. That shell is your ego, your mask, your character. That's what I meant by fighting your ego, not to allow it to obstruct your own growth.

"What's stopping you from your own molting process? The fear of change. You've heard me speak again and again of how important it is to change. Yet you and many others fear change, and you wish to control, down to the minute detail, every aspect of your life. Stop resisting and surrender. Nothing bad is going to happen. Let go.

"Give your ego a chill pill. It's this theme that is repeating itself. These fear-based thoughts aren't real. It's like a child being afraid of the boogeyman in the closet. Reduce it to that logic. When you shed light on what you think that fear is, it's no longer something you fear. What I'm saying is that it's time for you to look at your fears. It's time to look at your shadows.

"It's time to ask yourself, what things are you running away from? What things do you keep to yourself instead of showing them to the world because you believe that if you did show them, then somehow you'd be punished in some way? Punished in the form of loss–loss of friendship, loss of integrity, loss of people looking at you in a certain way, and loss of whatever status you think you have. All of what I just mentioned is based on how other people view you–again you take the utmost importance in all of this. You need to decide. Who do you want to put first? Yourself? Or everybody else? Now that doesn't mean that you're not open to ideas. That doesn't mean that you can't listen to opinions and what others have to say. But if you favor doing things predominantly because you think you should or otherwise, you're not living the life you're meant to live."

"What if that entailed my job?" I asked, feeling perplexed and a little angry. "What do you want me to do? You want me to just stop working, quit my job and not pay my bills?"

The voice's response oozed compassion. "You sound as if you have no choice, dear one. There goes the victim mentality. You sound as if the only choice you believe you have is that you 'have to' stay in something that you don't have fun with, because if you quit it, there's no alternative. I'm simply saying that when you begin to understand the idea that you have the right to have fun, and that you can make a lot of money while having fun, you'll begin to expand your shoebox, and your world will expand with it.

"Remember, the walls are alive, and you don't have to move all of them at once to begin to expand your reality. There are certain walls–your current perceptions and understandings–that you can keep fixed for now. Begin to work with the expansion of the other walls, ones to which you're not so attached. In time, the shoebox will expand, and as you assimilate the new information and begin to change, then you'll come back to those initial walls, and it'll get easier for you to work with them.

"Slowly but surely, the way you see and understand your world will change to fit more of what you want. And you'll begin to say, 'You know what? I'm going to work, all right, and I'm going to pay my bills, and I'm going to make so much money. But I'm no longer going to work at things that aren't fun! I only want to participate in things that are fun! I know I'll be provided for, and I will be safe!'

"Your fear of losing is how society controls you. You've been fed the notion of material abundance again and again. You fell for it, and you felt that you couldn't exist without it. Now you have experiential knowledge of the fact that material abundance will never fulfill you. You're also beginning to realize and understand that being of service to others is most fulfilling.

"You're at this precipice where the choices and decisions you make will have far-reaching consequences. That doesn't mean it's a warning. It doesn't mean that something is going to go wrong if you decide to go down one path or the other. But it does mean that there's an opportunity for you, right now, to fundamentally begin to shift the rest of your life. But you need to decide which way you want to go. Do you want to stay where you're at and continue to make money and live life just like everyone else? Or do you want to try something new? You may not have facts in front of you about what it's going to look like, but you know deep inside that it's your calling?

"Now this doesn't mean you get to be reckless and give up all your worldly possessions, because you need them while you're in this physical body. You need them. It's about looking at it and going at it in a way that works for you, and, above all, it's about being mindful about what other people say, but not allowing what they say to override what you know is true for you. This is one of the most important things you're cultivating right now, and it's not the scenario of me versus them. It's not you against the world. It has nothing to do with that. It's about, do I live an authentic life that represents me or do I live a life that fits somebody else's idea of how I should live my life?

"You've been down this road, and this lifestyle is very predictable now, and that's why it's no longer cranking up. Your energy wants more. You know what? Your father keeps on coming up. He's being shown to me as someone who's intellectually very strong and very precise. Almost like a teacher. Someone who finds comfort in logic and reason verses comfort through emotion. But what I'm sensing more than anything else is that there's a very structured way of looking at the world that although it feels safe and secure, it's in many ways very rigid. Consequently there may be a tendency towards looking at things as black and white, and that's very constricting. It's good to have a structured way of thinking in some situations, but when it comes to living life, it's very limiting; it restricts you and keeps you stuck in a box.

"You're someone who wants to live outside the box in which you've been put. So, in some ways, your soul is rebelling. It's saying, 'I want more out of life than what I have right now.' And you wanting more is also a realization that whatever that more is to you, it may not be suitable for other people. That's the hook. Because that, my friend, is acceptance. That ... is approval. That ... is belonging. When you do things and people are proud of you, you feel accepted and empowered. But here's the catch: if you don't have that solidity, that stability, coming from within, coming from inside of you, then when those people go away, or when they don't have a nice word to say about you, you crumble.

"You've just learned a secret, and that is, that the answers that humanity is seeking are found in curves, not in straight lines. Remember what I told you this morning? I see lines. Very straight yet equally spaced lines. That's how you've been looking at the world up until now. That doesn't mean that this is how you'll be looking at the world moving forward. This is the root of what's happening to you, you're ready to break away from the conditioning and move forward as a leader of your own life.

"Your past was a training ground that prepared and equipped you for your next step, and now your leadership skills are being called upon. You're being asked to remember who you are. You're also being asked to become more grounded; let your roots grow deep into the ground. Meaning that you can have a lot of knowledge, but wisdom only comes with emotional experience. The knowledge and the emotional experience together give you wisdom. They give you roots to help you stand firm and grounded, so that you have no reason to fear the wind when it comes.

"In other words, in order for you to gain a certain level of awareness, you'll be thrown into certain scenarios and challenges. The path of gaining experiential, emotional knowledge may not unfold exactly as you imagine it, but with each challenge embraced, you'll come to discover new gifts and aspects of yourself that you would otherwise not have known you had.

"You need to decide whether or not you want to continue doing and living life in this same old way. Because–guess what–it's predictable now. It's all just a pattern that repeats itself. At least now you know that you've done it a thousand times already. You've learned it, you've picked up on the patterns, you've collected your equations, and now all you're doing is plugging it all back in and getting results. Material results. But like I said, you don't even have to think about it. This way of living is getting–how do I put it gently–boring. Doing something different requires thought and effort. With it, comes a certain amount of risk. You don't really know what the future holds. Nobody knows, and that's where trust comes in. That's where faith and belief in yourself come in. And this means acknowledging what you're feeling and letting that feeling guide you.

"It's normal for you to feel fear. I want you to hear this. There's not going to be a day when you're not going to feel any fear when change happens. It's normal. It means you're not comfortable with what's happening because you can't see the future. For the ego, that's scary, because ego is based on safety, which is based on predictability. Be the inventor of your own life. That's how they asked me to say this to you. Don't ask people for permission. I'm not saying that you walk around asking people for permission all the time; that's not what I mean. But when you look for other people's approval for the fundamental things that you do in and for your life that make you happy or not, then you make your life almost their responsibility, and not yours. Be responsible for your own happiness."

CHAPTER 18

INCREASE YOUR FREQUENCY

"You're doing very well," the voice continued. "You've already increased your frequency greatly. They're asking that you keep doing what you're doing. In other words, continue to let yourself be willing to change. Because your body, as it attempts to change and become lighter, it will speak to you. It will send you signals through sensations and feelings. It will begin to move away from certain behaviours and adopt new ones. You simply observe it and allow it.

"This is exactly what we've talked about earlier. You felt like getting back into shape, so you decided to play soccer again. From there, you allowed the universe to bring someone into your life who would bring you back to practicing yoga. As time passed, your mind began to slow down, and one day, you realized that you couldn't remember the last time you'd actually turned on your TV, or even listened to the news. You noticed that you'd been spending most of your days out in nature, that you've come to enjoy spending time alone, and you're traveling a lot. The quality of people around you changed to include more genuine people–high frequency people. Even the food you eat has changed. You've been eating foods that

127

are high in oxygen and are closer to the sun—nuts, greens and fruits, especially blueberries. You're consuming a lot of water, and you seek spring water that is alive and oxygenated.

"What else? You're sleeping more and resting more. You're making that a priority for a change. Have you noticed all those changes? They happened slowly and gradually right under your nose. You didn't sit down and tell yourself, 'I'm going to stop eating meat, and I'm going to start eating this or that.' It all happened naturally. That's why I'm encouraging you to take time to reflect and notice your behavior. Notice what your body is doing. Notice what your body is teaching you. Honor your body."

I interrupted the voice, asking him, "I didn't know I was increasing my frequency. How was I doing it? How do I continue to increase my frequency?"

"Keep listening to your body, and keep allowing more information to come to you and through you. You're breaking down your own barriers around what you think is possible. And as you do that, the body gets retooled and redesigned to your new belief—to your new operating system.

"You're learning to live differently and to discern by the feeling in the center portion of your body. Your job right now is to make sure that you don't stop your evolution process, which you could do, because you have free will. Free will is the reason why you want to pray. Praying is nothing more than asking for guidance from whoever's listening. And by asking for help, you're allowing them to come and help. Free will is a double-edged sword; no one can hurt you unless you allow them to, and no one can help you unless you invite them to. That's what praying is all about. It's about asking, acknowledging and then allowing.

"Keep yourself in balance, and, by all means, call out through prayer or through intention, whichever feels more correct to you; call out what you desire. Before you eat, you can ask/pray/intend that the vibrations of what you place into your body become harmonious with your own vibe, and assist you in your own health and growth. Yes, that's why some religions teach you to pray before you eat. It's nice to begin to understand what you're doing, rather than just doing it because that's what you've been told to do, isn't it? Good times are ahead, dear one.

"You can make this easier for yourself right now. Rather than trying to understand why all this is happening and why I'm giving you this massive download today, rather than preoccupying yourself with this now–which isn't going to solve anything–why don't you do exactly what we've been talking about all day and develop trust in what you're feeling? Because that's your greatest ally. That's what guides you, what shows you exactly the direction you may want to take.

"That aspect of you, the perceiver, sees your life much more clearly and much more broadly than you in your current state with your physical limitations. When you listen to your intuition, the dude inside, you can hear him saying, 'Hey. I know your plan. Stop fighting. Just go with the flow.' Don't worry at all, but if you do, try to worry less about the stuff that really doesn't matter right now, because that's where you get stuck.

"The next time you have this feeling of I want more from life. Ask yourself, 'What do I want? What do I look forward to?' Your heart will tell you very loud and clear. And then acknowledge what the answer is for you. You don't have to act and do anything right away. At that point, you're no longer in denial, at least. You're being true to yourself.

"And then the next question to ask yourself is, 'What am I prepared to do to take this first step forward?' Make it a logical step, one that's doable, one that's feasible. Set yourself up for success. You can only do it one step at a time–and you learned that going up Mount Kilimanjaro, didn't you?" the voice added with a smirk.

CHAPTER 19

HONOR YOUR VEHICLE

The voice faded away, and I spent the next hour or so enjoying the scenery and digesting all the information I'd received. Through the bushes and trees, I saw another waterfall, and when I made it through the greeneries, I was surprised by the beauty of this hidden gem. I'd been walking for a while at this point, so I decided to lie down on a fallen tree.

As I lay down on my back and gazed at the sky, the voice found its way to me again. "Don't you find it interesting that you practice yoga?" he asked, and then followed it with, "Have you noticed that it was around the time you started yoga when all these changes started for you? Do you know what you were doing back then, during your practice?"

"After my classes I simply felt energized, clear headed, and had a lighter state of being," I replied. "I don't know why or how. I'm actually curious now. What was my yoga practice doing to me?"

"From a physical body point of view," the voice replied, "you were opening up and aligning energy channels within your body that have been clogged and dormant. That's why you always felt energized after your sessions."

131

"Energy channels? I have energy channels in my body? Why were they clogged? I don't get it."

"Here's how you can look at it. Imagine yourself walking into an old abandoned house that was once yours and was flourishing back in its days. You've decided to come back and live in it again. As you walk around the house, you start to clean the cobwebs and examine what's still working and what needs fixing. You find yourself attempting to open one of the water faucets, and you hear a loud squeaking noise.

"You quickly realize that if you're to come and live in this house again, in a way that meets your standard of living and taste, then you're going to need to completely renovate the house, and redo all the plumbing. And so, you start. It seems like a lot of work initially, and it goes very slowly. To top it all off, you start to experience all sorts of physical pain and exhaustion. Slowly but surely, though, you find that the pipes are running again, the lights are on, the house is waking up and feeling more alive. The house is your body, dear one.

"This is a small portion of what your asana practice was doing. There's a lot happening–it's an entire technology in and of itself–but ultimately, at the very base of your practice, what you're doing is focusing on and aligning with your breath. You're breathing. You're oxygenating your body. You're bringing in oxygen to all the different parts of your body that might not have been receiving proper oxygen throughout the day due to your daily postures.

"You hadn't focused on the breath enough. There are many ways to oxygenate the body, but breathing is your key. Whatever you're going to add to your life, utilize the great process of breathing. What do you all have in common with one another throughout the entire planet? Your need to breathe. And what does oxygen do to your system? In simple layman's terms, it regenerates. It activates what is going on inside of you."

Unsure of his meaning, I frowned. "Activates what's going on inside of me?"

"Think of yourself as a torch. When the batteries running the torch are fully charged, the torch is bright and powerful. When the batteries are low on charge, the torch will still function, but not to its fullest potential. Now imagine that the torch you've always had was running on low batteries your entire life; you wouldn't know its full potential. You'd believe that that's all your torch can do. This is what oxygen does to your body: it recharges your batteries so to speak, so you can begin to tap into your full potential."

"Are you serious?" I asked.

"Your modern-day scientists have caught up with what the yogis of old have known about conscious breathing, about the vital physiological benefits that come from it," the voice said. "I emphasise, however, that, ultimately, it helps refine your nervous system–the conveyor of information."

"Holy moly!" I exclaimed. "Why don't I already know about this! How do I add more oxygen into my body?"

"Like I said before, there are many ways to add oxygen to your system. You can ingest foods that are rich in oxygen, but the simplest approach is to become consciously aware of your breath. Through breath, you can do much more than oxygenate the body and activate your own self. You can also bring about a state of great calmness.

"In this time of transformation, I also suggest that you be kinder to your body. Drink plenty of water. Practice what we've just talked about–oxygenation and breathing–on a daily basis. Stretch or move the body in some way that acknowledges the energy moving through your body. I want to clarify the reason why I keep on emphasising the importance of your body. Early on in our conversation, I told you that the process of transformation starts with the mind. It's true. However, the mind and the body are interconnected. When you work on one, you affect the other.

"They are both independent, yet dependent on one another at the same time. Both need to have the capacity to support one another. It's an ongoing dance. You're a techie, so I want you to think of the mind, and the body, as the operating system or software and the actual hardware of your laptop, respectively. Now, if you want your laptop to do more things and have new features/capabilities, then you'd want to upgrade the software on your hardware. Once the software is upgraded, the computer (body) is capable of doing more than what it was capable of before. Eventually, there'll come a point where the new software updates are demanding more resources than what the current hardware can handle.

"At that point, you want to upgrade your hardware/computer to be able to support the needs of the new software. This dance between the mind and body continues. When I told you that you're powerful beyond measure, I wasn't trying to boost your morale. I'm very serious. This is why it's important for you to be kinder to your body and take care of it and listen to what it tells you. Remember when you reread that book a few years later and was mind blown that you only truly understood it the second time around? You simply had more capacity to process the data in that book. You see? It's a dance. A very subtle one.

"Now, undeniably, it can be a challenge to juggle your packed daily agendas and fit in all the things that you want to be doing. But you're learning how to love yourself and always do that which makes you feel good first. That does mean that you go ahead and eat an entire jar of Nutella. Although, that will definitely make you feel good, I want you to connect with the word 'feel' at a deeper level—at the level of the 'inner voice' that tells you what you really need and want to do for your overall well-being. I'm not taking about ego-driven desires that mask what you know is good for you at a deeper level. I'm talking about that voice that tells you to work-out, for example, because you know it will make you feel good.

"It doesn't mean that it has to be the first thing you do in your day. It simply means that you make it a priority that at some point during the day, you will honor your physical vehicle. That means to dedicate time during the day to practice any breathing technique you enjoy, to eat properly, to exercise, to meditate and to utilize your physical vehicle in a proper way. You want to make those things come first, and as you do those things on a regular basis, you'll find that you'll have a greater state of energy. As you begin to bring about this greater state of energy, you'll find that it's not necessarily coming from food but from breathing, meditation and being aligned with your thoughts and the changing of your beliefs (your upgraded software). You'll eventually conclude that the body doesn't have to be based on what your mainstream nutritionists say it should be.

"Next time you practice yoga. Before you go to your class or before you begin your practice, pose a question in your mind and then let it go, just let it go. Make it a simple one, not a complicated question. Make it simple. Could be as simple as, 'Please show me my next step.' Then just let it go, and then do your practice and notice when it comes to you. Remember, you're aligning with your breath so that your mind doesn't take over. It's calming down the chatter in your mind. You might notice that when you're in practice you're clearly hearing the dude inside, because you're much more in tune. In tune just enough to hear the answers. Because I want you to see, once again, how many of the answers that you're looking for are already inside you. You're just not practiced enough to look inside. Like most of the people in this world. It's just a matter of time before you awaken to your true nature.

"As you practice what we just talked about and allow yourself to listen and not be controlled by your past or by your future–even if you start doing that for only a few minutes every day–you'll allow yourself to clean and transform your old habit patterns and ways of thinking; aka you're saying good-bye to the old and outdated software you once had and getting closer to the dude inside, to the content creator within you that's waiting to be expressed."

CHAPTER 20

FALL IN LOVE WITH YOURSELF

"It's getting dark," the voice noted. "Let's start heading back and get ready for tonight's Ayahuasca (A South American entheogenic brew) ceremony."

The light in the forest was indeed growing dimmer. I didn't want to be caught in the jungle in the dark, so I turned and began to retrace my steps along the path.

"Speaking of which," the voice continued, "I want you to keep a journal and write about all your Ayahuasca journeys. That way you can go back to them at a later date. You might find you'll learn something new each time you go over them. All day we've been dancing around the answer to your question, "What is my next step?" To make it crystal clear: your next step is to allow yourself to love yourself more. Fall. In. Love. With. Yourself. Falling in love with yourself is the process of increasing your frequency. All these changes in your behavioral patterns–what you allow to enter your body and who, how and where you spend your time–are all geared towards increasing your frequency and becoming less dense.

"So, yes, look in the mirror and literally fall in love with yourself. Imagine that you're the significant other that you're falling in love with, and make a list of all the wonderful qualities you have, and keep adding to that list. As you practice doing that, you're going to learn about all the aspects of you that make up who you are as a whole. From there, many answers will be revealed to you. See ... this is what your last Ayahuasca ceremony was about. Do you remember it?"

"Of course, I do!" I grinned with enthusiasm as I recalled that journey. "It started off with an image of a human-like being, just randomly standing there in the middle of a pitch-black room, and its color started to change from gray into a colorful being. That being was then in a perpetual state of happiness, dancing and singing. From there, that being infected the one next to it, and slowly, one by one, an entire group of them went from gray beings into colorful beings.

"The vision then took me to another pitch-black area where I saw the same thing happening with another human-like being and group. The color spread like an infection from one place to another, but I couldn't see the bigger picture at that point. I could only see darkness everywhere and colorful light displacing certain patches. As the vision pulled me away from it, I slowly started to see the entire picture. It was still blurry, but I started to see that those beings in their groupings together looked like an organ. They looked like a massive human organ. But it didn't stop there.

"The vision pulled me even further out, and in the vastness of what seemed like outer space, I slowly but surely began to see more and more organs until I finally saw how all those organs came together. Just like the groupings of the smaller beings who came together to form an organ, the organs themselves came together to create this one massive humongous human body–relative to that initial human-like being. In that moment, I skipped a beat. Because that was when I realized that what I saw initially–a normal-sized human being–was merely a billion folds magnified point of view."

The voice chimed in, saying, "Those hundreds of billions of smaller beings that you saw, dear one, are the hundreds of billions of cells that make up your body. They are as alive and as conscious as you are. That's why they looked like humans in the vision, so you could connect the dots. The grouping of those smaller human-like beings represented tissues, and the other different groups represented different types of tissues, and together they all made up the healthy (colorful) organ you saw. As one organ received the colored light and began to function properly, it began to transmit light, and share this light (information) with the rest of the organs."

"Oh, yeah, that explains the change in color and the livelihood of those beings!" I responded.

"Yes, dear one! Organ by organ, they all fought the darkness, and they shared their light. How? Simply by allowing information (frequency/color) to come through, and then anchoring that frequency. From there their next step was to express their authentic truth, aka to broadcast that frequency, broadcast that knowing. Also, notice, when the organs had received light, they were finally able to see one another, for what and who they really are. They were able to see themselves in one another and finally understand one another, rather than fear one another. That was when they were capable of communicating clearly with one another."

"Right! That was when the much bigger being, the human that they made up, began to thrive. And it, too, changed its color and started to dance. I remember seeing that massive being looking like a massive robot with the many, many beings that made up that figure also dancing within that figure. Everyone and everything were dancing. There was so much color, so much happiness, so much excitement. I felt great after that Journey." Remembering it made me feel nostalgic.

If I could have seen a face for the voice, I think he would have smiled as he continued, "The much bigger being is dependent on the organs (grouping of beings) functioning together as one cohesive unit, dear one. A unit that knows that although it's made up of many different pieces that come in different shapes, forms and colors, all those pieces, in their essence, are the same. Each piece plays a unique role in allowing the much bigger being to function optimally. Now this awareness of unity started within one organ, but it didn't stop there. Did it?"

"No it didn't," I replied. "In that altered-state journey, the vision continued to pull me even further and further away from what initially seemed to be a humongous human figure (body). That figure eventually looked exactly the same as the human-like being I saw in the beginning. The further I drew away from what I saw, the more perspective I gained. I began to see the much broader picture, the much broader reality. I began to see and feel how it's all connected. How what one person does, affects the other."

"Yes, dear one. You are all connected. But not everyone is aware of it just yet. Similar to those cells and organs, you, too, are a part of a much bigger collective. As the vision continued to pull you even further out, the Earth, too, was shown as a cell relative to its galaxy, and it looked exactly the same as that initial human-like being. I'm sure you've picked up on the pattern already. The further out the vision took you, the more you were able to see all the galaxies, and just like the billions of cells that make up your body, the universe is made up of billions of galaxies.

"Can you see now what that vision was teaching you? It was showing you a universe within you that reflects the universe outside of you. You realized the illusion and the play in scale, micro vs macro, and how that affected your perception of all you see outside you. You're understanding now that all you see around you, right now, with your naked eye, in your perceived world, is simply a magnified image of all that is, and that there's much more to it all." The voice sounded optimistic as if buoyed by my growing understanding.

140

He continued, "By allowing light (information) to come to you and grow within you, you begin to see what you couldn't see before. With this clearer picture and knowledge, you automatically find yourself moving towards love, self-love and service. That's what that human-like being was doing. By serving itself, finding its way out of the darkness and falling in-love with itself, it began to express itself authentically. It began to dance and spread its light (broadcast its frequency). Light is information. Yes, it began to live a life of service.

"So you see ... being of service is the ultimate healing of the self. I know that when you find yourself involved in an act of service, it seems as if you're helping others, but when you're involved in service, you're really involved with the ultimate healing of your own soul. Because now you understand the oneness of being. Just like when those cells and organs began to see one another for who and what they really were, they were finally capable of understanding one another. That was when they began to function as a unit. Why? Because now they can see themselves in one another, and that made it easier for them to understand that they are all one.

"The main theme of that vision was unity, and the main message was about love. There's only one lesson to be learned, and that one lesson is love. In that vision, you had a taste of the inter-connectedness of all things. You're seeing clearly that the universe is within you. The cells in your body represent the entire human species. Your body is the entire universe from your cell's perspective. You're seeing the divine order within the chaos. You're seeing the pattern within the pattern within the other pattern ... from macro to micro from micro to macro.

"Just like the cells that make up the tissues that make up the organs that make up your body–your temple–this living breathing organism that you call human body, Earth is also one living breathing organism itself. Earth does not belong to you. Earth is also your temple. You belong to Earth. I think it's clear now that Earth is a sentient being. It's as alive and as conscious as you are. Mother Earth is what makes your experience possible. You've finally come to the realization that Earth is not something that you simply build upon, walk upon and take for granted. Up until that day, you didn't yet love Mother Earth enough or acknowledge her.

"Similar to the cells and organs. The humans that make up the countries are in their essence the same. They're not different at all. It's simply their culture medium (atmosphere) that makes their physicality/form look different. And because they identify with their form, and other labels, they perceive each other as different, and as such, see each other as separate. It's that identity crisis that we've talked about again and again.

"Humans battle and compete against one another because they've been kept from understanding one another. In ignorance they push back on one another and fight to defend their point of view, rather than opening up to one another and seeing the world through the other person's eyes. They can always choose to seek a solution that honors all, but here's the thing, they're not even aware that they're doing that, and they're not even aware that this is happening to them. They simply follow what others tell them and react to their environment.

"You're learning that the differences that you perceive are learned differences. They are cultural learned differences. I can hear you asking me, "Who taught us these differences?" It doesn't matter. What matters is to understand that none of you are different. None of you are separate from one another. The good news is, you're getting over that. The age of information is upon you. Information is light. Light is here. Where there's light, darkness disappears. That was another message in that vision. When a seed of light is implanted within you, there's no going back. Where there's light, you can finally see what has been right in front of you all along. I mean literally right in front of you all along. Keep learning and keep sharing information, and the understanding of one another will manifest itself.

"Did I mention that the work you're here to do is with the self? As you continue to work with the self and transform your thoughts, you'll change and transform your world as you know it. You literally jump realities. I told you many times, you're working with yourself and not others. I said this to you before; the ultimate truth that you're attempting to understand now is the absolute truth of yourself. The absolute truth of you. You're getting to know the self and most importantly how to allow information (light) to be housed within your body.

"In other words, you're learning how to be a frequency keeper, who lets that information be dispersed—or this frequency of yours be broadcast—by living, by being and by expressing your authentic self. You become a catalyst, simply through your 'beingness' and not through waving flags at one another.

"That's what that spreading of light was telling you in that vision. You think you must take care of others to be of service. But again, service truly means taking care of yourself and of your own body, because that's your concern. We've talked about that and about placing yourself first through value, not through selfishness. Whenever you find yourself putting into your life anything that doesn't keep you happy, it's because you don't value who you are. What do you end up doing when you don't value who you are? You settle for less. Why? You settle for less because you're afraid that if you don't settle for less, you'll end up with nothing. That's a belief, that's a fear, and a program you've accepted over and over again. The new generations are not going to get involved in that belief, because they know they don't have to settle for less, and they will teach their parents.

"As you and others learn to allow information and experiences to enter into your reality, you grow telepathically. You affect those around you in your friend groups, communities and then, of course, within your world. Just like the light spreading in that vision, what

143

will eventually happen is what you call critical mass. Where a certain number of individuals will achieve a certain state of knowing, and because of them, others will instantly comprehend. The more individuals who achieve this state of knowing, the more they'll tilt the odds of the bigger being in that vision coming back to light–moving from darkness and grogginess into the state of knowing and perpetual happiness and dancing.

"Imagine yourself trying to attract a piece of metal with a magnet. If you had a small magnet and you tried to attract a massive piece of metal, it's not going to work. If you had a massive magnet, then you'd find it easy to pull in that piece of metal. Think of thoughts and beliefs as a magnetic field. Like we've established, the bigger magnet (collective) is capable of influencing and attracting that tiny piece of metal. Up until this movement towards a universal knowing, the number of people who were in darkness was much larger than those who were aware and awake. As such, the dominant magnetic field was that of ignorance–not knowing what is–coming from their own thoughts and beliefs.

"Yes, they are 'telepathically' influencing all of humanity (the collective). Yes, without knowing, that state of being (ignorance) became the norm to them. Just like waking up and doing the same thing again and again. The rest (independent thinkers) were like the small magnet, to survive and to protect their magnetic field, they moved farther away, where there were no electromagnetic interferences influencing their thoughts. Some simply learned how to strengthen their own magnetic field and how to protect themselves. Yes, most people are worried about catching germs that are flying in the air, when, in reality, they want to shield themselves from thoughts that are flying in the air.

"What's happening right now is that more and more powerful individuals are being awakened. Those who influence others, whether in the media or otherwise, have awakened in the recent decades. More

144

and more are being awakened. The number of people who are meditating and allowing light, information and other frequencies to come to Earth has increased tremendously. Because of their own inner knowing and work within themselves, and with the changing of their own thoughts and beliefs (aka upgrading their operating system), they are supporting the collective.

"They're 'telepathically' broadcasting this state of knowing just by being and continuously working on themselves. This is why it's getting easier to accept and understand information that previously would've been rejected, ignored and labeled. This is what I meant by when I said that eventually you'll reach critical mass where this new, yet ancient information will become the norm again. Yes, similar to you, Earth is also going through its molting process.

"The existing structures are not capable of supporting who humanity is becoming. The change in humanities belief system (operating system) requires new structures (hardware) that can support who and what humanity is becoming. As such, you can see many changes occurring and many more will occur. This is not so different from the change that you've been going through. The work that you've been doing within your body and mind. Now, it's simply a collective body and mind. Remember ... you are part of a much bigger collective. And now you're understanding why I keep on telling you that you do your greatest work with yourself and not others. You serve others by serving yourself first. Again, no need to wave flags at other people. Now you can see clearly how when you work on yourself and with your thoughts, you upgrade your software and you affect the much bigger collective. This is how you can be of service to others.

"The more of you who learn to allow information to come in, house it and then disperse and share it, the more of you will be capable of understanding one another, and the more you will be capable of understanding yourself, as well. Key word, capable. It's not that you don't want to work together, you simply haven't been capable of it yet. Why? Because all kinds of precautions are being taken, and things being said, to keep you from discovering what you all have in common. This is changing now, as information (light) continues to spread.

"With information you'll fight separation–when you understand one another, separation (the grayness) will vanish because you'll no longer fear one another. Fear is simply lack of love, lack of light, lack of information. That's fear. It's the most ancient of all illusions. The source of it is lack of information. Lack of information causes misunderstanding and separation, because when you're afraid of something, you tend to push it away. When humans crack the code and truly understand what love means, and how it works, they'll transcend separation and it will be very clear to them that they are one. I'm taking every and any opportunity I get to convince you, that the system of the universe (you), exists as a single perfect organism. As one. You. Are. It.

"Now you're understanding what I meant when I said, 'Fall in-love with yourself.' It's not in the limited, materialistic and narrow point of view of you buying things, pampering yourself and putting yourself first. When you understand that you are all one, you begin to understand that you can't hate another human without hating a portion of yourself. You can't judge another human without judging a portion of yourself. Most importantly, you can't be fully in love with yourself if you have no love for other portions of you, aka other humans. Does falling in love with yourself make more sense now?"

I nodded and strode on back towards my hut as the voice continued: "It's the kind of love where, again, you fall in love with yourself through value not selfishness. Falling in love with yourself is the act of becoming whole. Now maybe the word holiness makes more sense to you. Love yourself and anchor that frequency (color) and then broadcast it for all to enjoy. Again, it's the only lesson that humanity is here to learn. Love."

CHAPTER 21

INFORMATION GATHERING SPECIES

I turned a corner on the path and looked up in surprise. "Oh wow, there's the hut. We're already back?"

"Yes. You see?" the voice said, "There was no need to be afraid earlier this morning when we started the walk. Yes, it was scary not knowing where you were going initially, but when you relaxed enough and allowed yourself to go with the flow, and be curious, you ended up enjoying your day. And look, you somehow found yourself back home. Like I said, it's always shaky in the beginning, because there's a lot of uncertainty, but as soon as you develop faith and trust in yourself, you begin to enjoy your journey, just like you did today."

"Look around you," the voice suggested. "Can you see now why you're out here in the jungle? Earth is your living library. From the birds singing this morning to the insects, the plants, the soil, the rocks, the trees and the streams of water, all things are purposely designed to hold knowledge. You, in your essence, are an information gathering entity. That's what this whole human experience is about. Mother Earth is literally a storehouse of information that's abundantly available to everyone.

"Your body is designed to be a vehicle that will allow you to experience this information. Yes, information is to be experienced through the framework of your own body. That's how you gain and anchor pure unfiltered knowledge from within, and how you transcend all mystery. And that's also why I keep on reminding you, again and again, to listen to your body. Because this is how you anchor your understanding, through experiential knowledge, and not from listening to what others tell you, or what others attempt to convince you of.

"Experiential knowledge empowers you. Can you see it now? Many of the answers you seek are being reflected back to you in nature. Like that mirror we talked about, you're just not looking in and at it. Why? Because your thoughts are taking you everywhere between past and future, but not right here and now. Remember that weird-looking tree? Where one stem forked out into many other aerial roots? And how each aerial root split even further apart into many other roots? One stem forking into many roots and then many roots and branches coming back to one stem? Look at the trees, they have so much to teach you."

I glanced at the trees as I clambered up the final slope to get to the hut.

"The stem supports its branches and the branches support their offshoots. The offshoots support the leaves, and each individual part grows independently, yet symphonically with the whole. Observe the animals. Observe the plants. Learn from the flowers. Learn from the insects. We went over a simple example with the bee and the flower earlier. It's all in front of you, eagerly waiting for you to get out of your head, get curious about life, and begin to dare to ask questions.

"Just like the streams you bathed in today, you, too, have rivers of water flowing through you. I want you to see and understand that you and Earth are not so different. Just like Earth is mostly covered with water, you, too, are mostly water. Yes, it's the same pattern I keep

148

mentioning to you in hopes that one day you'll understand that all that exists outside of you is merely a reflection of what's happening inside you. Meaning, if you can tap into a pattern or understanding of what's happening within yourself, within the framework of your own body, then you can tap into an understanding of the macro scale, the entire universe.

"You can think of yourself as a water being. What is water after all? It's a supreme channel of sound and vibration, and it, too, is living and conscious."

I stepped onto the platform that made the floor of my hut and flopped onto the bed. I was getting hungry and thinking about food, but all sorts of electrical impulses fired in my head like fireworks, and I remembered an awesome documentary I'd watched about water. That documentary had opened my eyes at the time. It pulled information from many different scientific researchers coming from all walks of life. It reinforced an experience I had back in Mount Shasta, California. It spoke of water and how the vitality of water depends on how it flows or how it's forced to flow. Yes, water can die if it's treated poorly. It also talked about how the current human systems that are in place treat water as if it's merely a fluid without life or energy, and so they force water to flow along straight and rigid shapes that are never found in nature. Those systems ignore water's natural rhythm, natural path, and, as such, the natural structure of water breaks down more and more by the time it gets to your house. Meaning that the water that reaches your house is not necessarily alive.

The voice interrupted my replay or that documentary, saying, "Yes. You want to provide the opportunity for water to breathe. You want to allow it to energize and oxygenate itself so it can remain alive. I'm talking about you, dear one. Notice how the same human systems treat you just like they treat water. Pressuring you in the kindest and subtlest of ways to live in rigid straight lines, narrowing your creativity and vision, as if you're merely a machine. They condition you to live in the future, which we've already established doesn't exist until you create it. That way of living goes against the law of nature where a 'human being' is meant to simply BE as one moment unfolds into another.

"Living against the natural rhythm of you creates dis-ease. It also creates the need to control what cannot be controlled. The latter creates anxiety that is sourced from the fear of not knowing what tomorrow holds. This is a vicious cycle of fear that you lock yourself into. This fear, in which, over thousands of years, the human race has become acclimatized to live in, has become the norm. You're moving away from that, because now you have information; now you have knowledge, and with it comes power, and with power comes sovereignty. That will be the frequency that you'll be sending out the universe–the frequency of self-liberation, the frequency of love.

CHAPTER 22

A DIFFERENT DIMENSION

"You can clearly see now," the voice went on, "that the ultimate subjugation of humanity was never really from the use of physical weapons. It comes from the very subtle psychological manipulation of consciousness. Those who exist within it don't even realize they're in prison ... Now, light up the candle before it gets pitch-black and you can't see anymore."

I did as the voice suggested and as soon as the candle flared into life, he gave further instructions:

"Take a closer look at that candle, and observe the flame. Observe closely. The heat from the first flame melts the wax near the wick. That liquid wax travels up the wick and gets vaporized by the heat. Now these vaporized molecules react with the great and almighty oxygen from the air to create heat, light and other byproducts. The combustion process goes on, again and again in great rapidity. One flame after another—cause, effect, cause, effect. A cause generates an effect, and that effect turns into a cause, which generates another effect, and all of it takes place at such high speeds that it deceives your eyes and makes you think it's the same solid flame.

But it's never the same flame, and that flame is far from being solid.

"You're learning now what your scientists concluded decades ago and what indigenous cultures and enlightened individuals concluded thousands of years ago. And that is that the third-dimensional experience seems to be solid and very well defined, when in actuality, it's all just flickering in and out so fast that you perceive it to be solid—just like you perceive this flame. You're moving into a different experience now. You're moving into a different dimension, one of perception."

I frowned. "Wait a minute. Did you just say a different dimension?"

"Yes, dear one," the voice replied. "You're moving into a dimension where you can perceive other frequencies, ones you were not able to tap into before."

"How does that work?" I asked. "Is the dimension you're taking about another place I could go to? And if I go there, what happens to this dimension that I occupy right now?"

"You are asking all the right questions, dear one!" the voice responded. "Dimensions are not places. They are simply states of being. They resonate within frequency ranges."

"Are you kidding me? Is this what this whole 'increasing my frequency' is all about?" I asked.

"Yes, dear one!" The voice sounded thrilled. "Like I said before, many more aha moments will come to you. Much of what we talked about today will make more sense in time. But for now, I want to clarify that although all dimensions are right here and now, one dimension has nothing to do with another. The only thing in common between dimensions is the observer of the experience.

"You're simply moving into a different vibrational state of being. There's no need to wave flags at others. Your only concern is to focus on you. Let everyone else be where they are and honor them, but your focus and concern, is you."

"Is this why you keep on telling me to take care of my body?" I asked.

"Yes, dear one. Your body is your temple. It's not you. Take another closer look at the candle. This flame gives birth to light, right? Now, as you can see with your naked eye, light has no form, although it comes from form. You, dear one, are such light. In form, in your body, you are tied down, just like the flame fastened to the candle. And just like the light coming from the flame, you, too, are in the process of changing forms. That's what you're seeking, though you don't know that you are. You're seeking freedom from bondage.

CHAPTER 23

IMPERMANENCE

Night was falling rapidly now, setting the candlelight in stark relief against the darkness, but still the voice continued:

"You're at the point where you're solidifying your understanding of this concept within the framework of your own body. You're doing this through your meditation and through observing sensations—vibrations—all over your body that tell you that you, and the world, are not the type of solid you always thought they were. You're more like a persistent flame (frequency) that's never the same, constantly changing and ever so impermanent.

"Yes, deep are the mysteries around you, and hidden are the secrets of old; but that, too, will change. Learn to feel what I'm saying, because that's what this is about—for you to feel what I'm telling you. Not for you to think it out and rationalize it. But to feel it. You are, as I always not so gently remind you, a result of your own thoughts. This understanding, this knowledge, is growing very deep within you at this time.

"Nothing is permanent. Just like that constant flickering flame. You've already changed since the time you and I started this lovely chat. Yes, you are a completely new person now; whoops, I'm talking to another you again. I'm emphasizing the notion because I want to address the concept of judgement again. I want you to notice how subtle it is and how often you unconsciously do it. It's time you let go of judgment–the judgment of others and self. Next time you run into someone you haven't seen in a while, notice if you're looking at the image your mind sketched many years ago, when you last met them, based on what they said or did then, or if you're looking at the person as they are and who they have become right now?

"The mind is an interesting creature. It immediately judges (sketches an image) the person it meets based on what it knows, based on the conditioning of its own culture medium and the beliefs collected from experience–none of which have to do with the person in front of you. It all has to do with you. Nevertheless, you address the image that you sketched of that person–and how you think they should be–not the person who's talking to you in that present moment, as they are right there and then.

"You're understanding now the importance of taming the mind and how the mind can swiftly take you away from the moment you want to experience. Whenever you meet with someone, even if you see this person every day, let go of the image you have of them and meet them for the first time again and again. This way you're actually keeping up with who they're becoming and not with who they were. This is living in the now. This is escaping the mind. Soon this way of living becomes a portion of your beingness.

"At this stage of our interaction, you're also solidifying your understanding of how the future really works. It's in a state of constant change. All there is, all that exists, lies in the present moment of experience, where that flame comes to life. That moment will unfold continuously into another moment–another flame. Cause and effect ... just like the flame you see. Constant cause and effect, one after the other. How did it all start? It all came from the first cause. Which

156

was the lighting up of the candle, which was caused from a thought that you had. In plain English, you are the cause generating the effect, and that effect turns into a cause, which generates another effect. And all of it takes place at high speed, which creates your current reality.

"Yes, this is your video-content creation process. To control the future, which is what you keep on trying to do, all you need to do is consciously create a cause in the now. Create a cause in the present moment that will generate a desirable effect in a future moment. Just like that, you create your reality. Remember that the first thought arose from sensation, and the first cause came from that thought. So sensation is at the base of the mind. Study and observe sensations and notice what they're teaching you. That's the bottom line. Everything we've talked about today can be deduced from the latter.

CHAPTER 24

THE POWER OF THE WORD

"Speaking of sensation," the voice continued, "we mentioned earlier that you're mostly water. Water is very sensitive to what it encounters. Anyone or anything that comes into contact with water leaves a trace. That is why its character (ego) is influenced by the atmosphere (culture medium) where it flows. Water doesn't resist; it simply is. It goes with the flow. On its path, it collects and reacts to information from the air, the people, pollution, computers, television sets, microwaves, radio waves, cellphones and, yes, even words written on a piece of paper. All those frequencies influence water.

"I can feel some neurons firing in your head. You're beginning to understand why your body, which is mostly water, has been seeking some time alone, and why you've been spending most of your time in nature, away from the pollution of cities. You don't even remember the last time you switched on your TV–the primary tool used to manipulate your consciousness–or watched the news–another tool used to manipulate your consciousness. Your body, as it attempts to decondition you, is moving you away from frequencies that don't

159

serve you. Away from the frequency of chaos, anxiety, stress, and temptations of all kinds. Temptations that you don't need, that keep you away from staying clear and centered. That's why, here in the jungle, you're getting clear in the head, and you're listening to what's going on inside you. In other words, you're observing the world as it is, rather than getting lost in it.

"You are, and you have been, listening to your body. Keep doing that and you'll continue to increase your frequency. Can you see why I told you earlier that the words you speak to yourself solidify your experience? Ha! I love that smile on your face! It's all coming together now, isn't it?"

I chuckled at these words. The voice was right.

"The influences around you are very, very subtle. Something as simple as a letter in a word is powerful. Letters are shapes that have their own frequency; put a few of them together, and you create a word, a much-amplified frequency that has the ability to empower or disempower you. You can only imagine the power of a well-articulated sentence. That's why when someone doesn't know how to write a word, they ask, 'How do you spell it?' Yes, each and every word that comes out of your mouth is as powerful as casting a spell onto someone. Hopefully that logic puts things into perspective and helps you understand how powerful words are.

"That's why I told you earlier to be careful how you speak to yourself. Be careful how you speak to others as well. Even your scientists have shown, after performing many tests with water, that water crystals change forms under the influence of frequencies–including words and the intention behind those words. Remember, you are mostly water. Most importantly you're learning that under the influence of frequency, a transformation of matter occurs."

CHAPTER 25

TRANSCENDENCE

The voice stopped speaking, allowing me time to reflect on his words. My mind roamed back to the start of my journey, when I first let go.

The first country I found myself visiting was Peru. In 2016 I started to feel Peru drawing me in like a gigantic magnet pulling a tiny piece of metal towards it. There was a sense of inevitability to it. I simply knew that I needed to be there–though I couldn't rationalize it.

Two years later, I made it, and after a few days trekking through the Andes, I developed a friendship with the local guide. One day as we talked over dinner, I found myself asking him about Ayahuasca.

His eyes opened wide. He looked at me in a strange way and said, "Why do you ask...? Do you want to do Ayahuasca? It's not good for you."

Surprised by his reaction, I told him the truth, that I knew nothing about Ayahuasca. I told him I was simply interested in learning more about it. I was curious about how it worked and what exactly it did.

It soon became clear to me, however, that he didn't have the answers I sought. He responded with a question, saying, "How did you hear of Ayahuasca?"

I told him that a friend of mine brought up Ayahuasca in a conversation when I mentioned I was going to Peru. That was the first time I'd heard about it.

The guide looked at me and said, "Well ... I know a guy who performs Ayahuasca ceremonies. He's powerful. I'll connect you with him."

We had that conversation at ten at night, but minutes later, I was on the phone with his friend–who ended up asking me the same question. "Why do you want to do Ayahuasca?"

I told him I was simply curious and wanted to learn more about this Ayahuasca that people talk about.

He challenged me with a series of questions, and I was about to hang up on him, when he said, "Your eyes will tell me everything I need to know. I need to look into your eyes, and I will get all the information I need. I'll meet you tomorrow at 7 am, outside the hotel in Lima."

Sure enough, the next morning at 7 am, he walked into the hotel. He was a short, dark-skinned, chubby looking kinda guy, but as soon as he walked into the reception and looked at me, I could feel his presence. We left the lobby and stood at the corner of the street outside.

He looked at me and said, "Relax."

In my head I said, I am relaxed.

He said, "You're not relaxed. If you were, I'd know."

Did this individual just read my thoughts? I wondered to myself.

He smiled at me and said, "Loosen up your arms. Loosen up your legs. Don't worry. Nothing wrong is going to happen." After I'd shaken my limbs a little, he continued, saying, "Look me in the eye, and tell me, why do you want to do Ayahuasca?"

"I really don't know," I replied.

He took a step closer to me and pierced my eyes with his gaze. I felt the power of it throughout my being. In a matter of seconds, he took a couple of steps back, and his bullish attitude of treating me like a white boy tourist wanting to try Ayahuasca suddenly turned into respect. He honored and acknowledged my presence, as if he knew who I was at a level I wasn't aware of at the time.

"Welcome home," he said. "I know you from before, brother. You don't need Ayahuasca. When you go to Lake Titicaca, make sure you keep a pen and a paper with you. Write down the guidance that you'll receive, and most importantly, do not question what comes through." He then left and that was the last I saw of him. I don't know his name. I don't have his contact info, and the guide I knew refused to give me this guy's contact info, as well.

After that conversation, I simply stood in silence, feeling the truth resonating throughout my entire being. I stood there in awe, paralyzed by what had just happened. I mean, I was literally paralyzed. I could feel what he said, but I couldn't put words to it. I just felt it. My mind, however, couldn't rationalize it and wanted to reject it because it went against its own conditioning.

At that point, I still hadn't connected the dots with my innate desire to visit the country in the first place. Many other experiences occurred around Ollantaytambo and other cities, but I won't go over them now. When I was there, I simply felt that I was home. Around that time, towards the end of 2018, I decided to sit down and write this book, and through my writing, I began to understand my experiences—none of which had been normal in the third-dimensional sense.

See … not too long before that experience, I was living the life of my dreams—or so I thought. I then began to experience another reality all together. It felt like I was in a Hollywood movie. Scratch that. More like a Bollywood movie. It still does, and it keeps getting more and more exciting. The main question I had at the time was 'who are all these people who keep on walking into my life, giving me a kind and soft slap on the face to knock some sense into me, and then simply walking away?' Who was that person to me? Why did he act so weird when he gazed into my eyes? What did he see? How did he read my thoughts? Why was my mind resisting all of this? Why was I so afraid of it all?

A few months, cities and countries later, I circled back to Peru. "There's something still to be learned on that piece of land," I said to myself.

This time I visited the other side of the country. A few hours out of Pucallpa, you'll find the jungle, and that's where I ended up. There's no cell service, no connectivity, no Wi-Fi, no nothing. It's completely off-grid and disconnected. I knew no one and didn't speak the language. What was I doing there?

The answer was clear: that's where I needed to be. I felt better as soon as I arrived there.

I got off the back of the truck and stepped into the heart of a small, remote community with a few simple huts and a *maloca*–a large, traditional Amazonian house at the center of the community where ceremonies take place. The village sat right next to a magical river. When I say magical, I mean really magical, not figuratively speaking. It truly felt like I was in the movie Avatar.

The trees, the plants, the water, the flowers, the insects were all so extremely alive. Untouched by humans. I was in another world all together. Freshest air I'd ever inhaled. Initially I planned to stay there for one week to explore Ayahuasca, and then I'd leave, but I ended up staying there for roughly a month. I would've stayed longer had I not figured out what was really going on over there.

Like I said, I didn't know anything about Ayahuasca at the time. I'm not one to learn simply by listening to what others have to say or through reading books and theories. I'm a hands-on learner type of guy. If I want to learn and truly understand something, I need to get my hands dirty and gain unfiltered experiential knowledge. I simply throw myself into it and learn as I make my way out of it. Once I'm done, I know the ins and outs of what I'm learning and experiencing. Then I enjoy teaching and sharing what I've learned. It's one of my strongest passions. I've operated like this since high school. It's also how I develop my inner self. Yes, this is why I wrote this book, too.

After a few days living in the community, I learned of an option to move to a Tambo—an isolated hut—in the jungle that's twenty to thirty minutes walking distance from the community. I decided to go ahead and do that. The first two nights, I was scared. It gets pitch dark at night, so dark you can't see fingers that are literally right in front of you. I mean, I held my palm a couple of inches away from my face, and I still couldn't see it. That's how dark it gets. I felt claustrophobic. My eyes were useless. At the same time, that's when the jungle woke up.

Everything from frogs, to bats, to insects, and all sort of creatures that I didn't know of came awake. It was very loud. The first night I lay on my mat under my mosquito net, I turned on my flashlight, looked up and saw a black Tarantula standing still on my net. It's fair to say that I didn't sleep well that night.

As the days passed, I began to experience more and more peace. I became more at ease with myself. I felt different. I felt calm and quiet. I spent most of my days by the river allowing the sun rays to energize my body, while simply observing my surroundings. I spent the many hours and days just resting and meditating in isolation. I'd never, in my entire life, felt so present and so in tune with myself and nature. I felt that I'd come home.

Fasting was interesting. Initially, I felt angry and agitated. Three days later, I decided to make my fasting even more severe. I began to experiment with myself. I began to simply notice that feeling of hunger when it hit, and then I sat with that sensation and made peace with it. I watched my angry thoughts. I then watched my body wanting to lose it. When it got really bad, I simply went and took a dip in the river and stayed there until I calmed down. I also went to sleep as early as possible before my hanger overpowered me.

I realized that those hunger patterns were disguising other inner patterns that were waiting for me to acknowledge them and heal them. That was when I tapped into this inner voice. I started to truly hear him clearly. After some proper/severe fasting–with only a few tablespoons of some unseasoned (tasteless) rice porridge in the morning–I had my first profound and vivid Ayahuasca journey. In that journey, I became whatever I was curious about. This was the main theme. I learned a lot about what compassion truly meant from that journey. I also learned a lot about desire.

One of the most profound lessons I've learned is that the body and mind need to be ready to receive these teachings. I learned that I needed to be at the same frequency as the information I was seeking. I didn't need to run off and go look for it outside of me. I simply needed to be prepared from within. Once I'm at the frequency of the information I am seeking, it automatically downloads, and information is exchanged. Now, that realization was mind blowing, yet at the same time a portion of me didn't feel as if I had learnt something new. It felt as if I had relearnt what I already knew deep inside.

The first teaching I received from an Ayahuasca journey started with sacred geometry that resembled geometry that I used to draw for fun, back when I was in high school. I learned that there was much more to those shapes than just fun. Out of nowhere, I found myself surrounded by colorful beings that looked like colored gas in human-like shapes. They were kind, soft, and so gentle and sweet. I felt nurtured in their presence. They kept saying, "We're always here ... Jump, we'll catch you ... Jump ... we'll catch you. We love you ..." I didn't understand what they meant at the time.

Next, all I could see was a green screen. I followed the color and travelled with it. It gave me power, it gave me strength, it gave me

166

material abundance, it gave me a crown and made me feel like a giant–everyone and everything else looked so tiny relative to me. I loved it. I desired more of it. I felt like I owned the entire world. I was so into the experience that I wanted to stay there. I craved it. Next thing I know, it was all taken away from me. Yes. Everything was taken away from me, and I felt weak and powerless. I felt the withdrawal in my physical body as well. It was painful. I felt nauseous.

I told myself wow, I know now that I shouldn't seek things from outside of me, especially the illusion that power comes from outside. I won't be tricked again. Then the screen turned blue. The blue color pulled me out of the gutter and gave me power, then more of it, and I loved it. I desired it, I craved it, and I wanted more and more of it. Yes, you guessed it. It was all taken away from me again. And, yes, I fell for it again! I felt sick and nauseous, and I asked them to stop tormenting me. But then I had a moment of clarity. I was tormenting myself.

I understood that it was only my own desire that brought me to my knees. See ... the influences are all around you, all the time. I mean all the time. They are potently subtle. It's only your own desire for them that allows you to give your power away to them. You can continue to seek outside of yourself and gain material things and power, but what if I took it all away from you? Who are you without it? What happens to you? Are you powerless? You become powerless because of your own belief. Your belief that your power comes from outside of you. In reality, your power, your divine power, lies inside of you. No one can take it away from you. It's already inside you. It's a matter of tapping into it, trusting it and beginning to use it. Now you know that no one can take your power away from you, and at the same time, no one can give you power.

Only you choose to give your power away to others, and things, outside of you. Why? Because you've been kept from finding out who you really are. Kept from finding out how powerful you really are. Come back to your center. From your center, you begin to tune into your own teachings, and no longer have to follow and learn from others. From that place, it's easier to take control over the mind and body's knee-jerk reactions. You slowly but surely become sovereign. You'll no longer live outside of yourself, mistaking your identity with someone or something outside of you. Now you can see that any teaching that points you to look outside of you is not for your highest good. Because if I, as an outsider, give you something, then I can also take it away from you. But if you, as an insider, can give yourself what you seek and want. Who is going to take that away? No one! Welcome to your innate power. Now that's sexy! That's independence!

When you tune in, you transcend your identity crises. You begin to understand that the material world is fun, cool and attractive, but there's a vast, more fulfilling and way cooler world inside you. That world can't be taken away from you. Spending your life collecting information and materials from outside of you, allowing them to define who you are, and being tricked into believing that you gain power by gaining more material stuff, this is how you're being duped. The word 'successful' dupes you, as you're continuously encouraged to collect fake power that is ultimately in someone else's hands. That's a massive illusion.

Every day you are continuously bombarded with influences, from the subtler ones to the most obvious ones. Now it's true that the influences are there, but if you're centered, you begin to acknowledge your desires without succumbing to them. Then these influences can't control you and make you their puppets. You simply become a witness, an observer, and then you act from a place of knowing. You act from a place of understanding, and not simply reacting and following desires and allowing them to override who you are. That's what I was practicing through my fasting without knowing that I was: practicing to tame my hunger, to observe the pain and not

168

turn physical pain into mental pain, to simply learn and take control over my body again, to transcend its habit patterns.

Back in that Ayahuasca journey, they were teaching me to look around me, to notice the influences, but to act from my center. I want you to sit down with this. Whether these desires were food, sex, material successes or whatever they are, I want you to sit down and notice and observe your blind habit patterns. Notice how quickly your desires turn into craving. Notice how that craving turns into clinging. The initial desire came from a sensation on the body, like we established earlier. Sensation comes from contact with your senses: eyes, ears, nose, tongue, body and mind. Influences come through visuals (what you see), smells (perfume), sounds (ear), tastes (tongue), touch (body) and thoughts (mind).

Most of the senses we talked about are easy to understand. Thoughts, however, I find interesting because they're not so obvious. The first challenge is to understand how your thoughts influence you. Next is to declutter your thoughts, find out which thoughts are really yours and which ones you have so innocently adopted without knowing. Thoughts travel telepathically. Like I said before, most of you worry about catching germs, when in reality, you want to be more aware of catching thoughts.

The more sensitive you become, the more you'll notice your body getting agitated when you're in a room with people whose thoughts don't vibrate at the same frequency as yours. If you don't have a strong magnetic field, and don't know how to protect yourself, then without knowing, you end up adopting those people's thoughts. Yes, you become like them. You begin to create a reality based on their collective psyche and not yours–all while believing that you're creating your own reality. You see. It's good to keep it simple and come back to the root cause, of where it all starts. It's good to get curious and ask questions. To study yourself. To know yourself.

I've been dancing around this long enough. See ... as long as there is contact, there is influence. There is always contact. Whether through your physical sensations or through thoughts flying in the air. The key is to learn how to turn sensations on the body from this cycle of craving and aversion into wisdom. This is how you transcend. I'll further clarify this. When you're playing one of those virtual reality games, it all feels very real, although none of it is happening. Why? Because the mind can't tell the difference. The virtual reality headset/mask overrides this reality. Meaning that the information you decode comes from contact with your senses.

Now this VR headset is hijacking the information you perceive. It gives you false data and information. Who processes this information? The mind. From there you begin to identify with that virtual reality, because that's the only information you're receiving. For now, I want you to assume a scenario where that headset is stuck to your head. In that case, you got so used to living in that virtual reality, and so stuck in it, that you believe it's real and that's all that exists.

The question is, how can you transcend and discern without removing the headset? That was the question for which I was seeking an answer. Now that I know that the information I receive isn't necessarily all true, I know I need to use more than just my sensory organs. My senses are pretty robotic. I mean, they have no discernment. They simply process and decode the signals that they're exposed to. From there you rationalize those signals.

Although that way of living is logical, but again now that I know the information I receive from the outside world is hijacked to a certain degree, I understand the need to use more than just logic to navigate my way through. The real question is, how do you transcend all of this? Are you ready for the answer? The answer is your heart.

Once again, I'm not talking about the physical heart; I'm talking about the energetic heart. The energy vortex, the chakra itself. It's not the distorted definition of love that's been marketed to you.

Love is a vibrational state of being. A very powerful state of being. That's why it is important to discern with the heart. Your heart is the key to transcendence. Your heart is a powerful tool. That energy vortex is connected to source. No VR tool can manipulate the information that comes straight from source. If you open your heart and use your heart's mind, then you begin to discern your surroundings and make decisions from a place of clarity, without the intervention of the influences that surround you.

The heart is much faster and wiser than the mind. Why? Because the mind in its conditioned state is always seeing things as black and white, right or wrong, good or bad—constantly labeling and judging anything that is not it as separate from it; and as such, remains off balance. With the eyes of the heart, all judgments disappear. Why? Because the heart is balanced by a deeper inner truth. Next time you think you are lost, take your question to your heart. It's not as hard as you think it to be. Simply follow the lightness in your heart and that will lead you to what you are seeking. That will lead you to your aliveness.

You become a perceiver and a feeler, rather than a thinker. You slowly begin to transcend illusion. The mind—especially when it's untamed—is dangerous. Imagine when it's constantly receiving fake data from this VR headset in our analogy? In that VR reality, you're constantly fed fear. Fear is an extremely low frequency. That's why you keep on fighting one another. That's why the differences between you all have been marketed to the masses: to keep you separated and to keep your heart centers closed. When in reality your heart center is your key. Use your heart's mind to make decisions, and then wake the mind up and get work done using the logical, analytical and systematic approach. You want to use both. Not just one or the other. You need both. That is power.

THEMINDCHEMIST

172

CHAPTER 26

SHAPESHIFTING

At that point when the colorful beings knew that I understood what they were teaching me, my journey shifted to another experience. I suddenly found myself experiencing being a plant. But not any plant. I became the plant I was looking at and had admired earlier that morning. It grew right in front of my tambo (hut) where I stayed. Here's what happened.

Earlier that morning when I stopped to admire this plant, I stepped on an ant. The reason I share this is because when I shapeshifted into the plant, I could see myself from the plant's eyes. I want to be very clear. When I say I became the plant, I truly embodied the plant. I was the plant itself. I could feel what she felt. Hear her thoughts. All of it. She had so much compassion for me. She didn't feel petty, but she did feel compassionately sorry for me. I heard her say to my human self–as I watched myself through the plant's eyes– "Sit still. Sit still. From there you can see ... From there you can see what I see".

Plants and trees, they laugh at us humans. I was able to feel what it was like to be completely still, to simply be and observe. To be

173

a part of the earth and to simply watch my human-self walking around in front of my tambo. I felt compassion for my human self as I watched him declutter all the conditioning and heal many wounds he wasn't aware of. From the plant's eyes I could see so much suffering. That was a fascinating experience, but it didn't stop there. While experiencing being that plant, I was shown the moment the plant observed me step on the ant. Just before I did that, I felt what the plant felt as she yelled, "No!" trying to warn me that there was the ant there.

In that moment, while I watched my human self just about to step on the ant, I shifted from being the plant to becoming the ant. Yes, I became the ant, and, when I saw that massive foot about to crush me, I felt sick to my stomach.

After feeling that pain, you could say I was scarred for life. In a good way. I can no longer hurt a single insect–no matter how scary they look because I don't understand them, and no matter how small they are. I don't have it in me to take that life away. To be able to experience that plant and that ant, and then, later, other animals, shook my reality. Being able to feel both of them made me truly understand how alive and conscious nature is. The trees, the rocks, the plants, the pebbles, the flowers, all of it. They are all as aware as you and I. If not more.

I also realized that I'm not to disturb the balance of nature. I'm simply to be in harmony with it all. As you can see, you can truly learn about compassion when you're able to become that thing or that person you're trying to understand.

When I realized and understood that I was living in the middle of a library (nature), I began to ask questions. The plants and trees taught me how powerful it is to sit in silence, and they showed me the clarity that comes forth from it. They simply intend to have water and food, and then it comes to them; they don't go running and fighting for things. They simply tune in, intend what they want and wait for it to come. That simple.

174

The more in tune I became with nature, the more sensitive I became. My awareness increased. I had no need or desire to speak much. Talking felt exhausting. I began to embody the teachings of nature subconsciously. I began to see clearly. I became a man of a few words, because I realized there's no need to speak more than the minimum necessary words to express myself and get my point across. I conserved a lot of energy that way.

CHAPTER 27

SUPREME CHANNEL OF SOUND AND VIBRATION

Now let's pick up where we left off with the voice back before the Ayahuasca ceremony.

After the voice emphasized the power of the word, I asked him, "What part did Ayahuasca play in my journeys? There's not a single doubt that Ayahuasca played an important role, but the question is, what did Ayahuasca do precisely? I feel like there were other factors in the mix, weren't there?"

The voice answered, "What did the shaman call himself? He called himself the maestro, the orchestrator. What did he use to 'hold space' during the ceremony? He used a powerful tool–his voice. Remember we said that water is a supreme channel of sound and vibration. Yes, you are a supreme channel of sound and vibration. That's why the shaman called himself the maestro, because he understood the power of his voice and what sound frequency can do to your mind, body, soul and spirit. Sound is a tool for transformation in and of itself.

"Each ceremony was different, although you were ingesting the same plant every ceremony. That's because in each ceremony, you

177

had different people (vibrational frequencies) joining the group, and in each ceremony, you had different Icaros (chanting). Have you noticed that the chanting itself always had a rhythmic pattern that endlessly repeated itself? And some people's chants gave you a sense of ecstasy, a feeling of blissfulness in the exact moment they started chanting. Those moments echoed the exact same feeling that you felt in those fleeting moments during your meditation. You were able to reach the same level of harmony within you, without any substance or sound, but it took you longer to get to that point through meditation only.

"Back to the ceremony. You could also feel how the shaman was commanding the space with his voice during his chants and how the chanting affected your emotion. That, my dear, was your first transmission of the power of sound, as something which transforms not just your emotions, but the very elements themselves. Like I said, you're learning that under the influence of frequency a transformation in matter occurs. Your scientists proved this by performing many experiments and collecting facts and, you know, all the logical stuff that humanity is addicted to. You have experiential knowledge of it! Now that's a whole new level of understanding that you truly are a supreme channel of sound and vibration. And your body is sensitive to the influences of your surroundings, no matter how subtle they are, even when you're not aware of them.

"I want you to notice what the shaman does during the ceremonial ritual. The ceremony begins by spreading the smoke of burning incense in the *maloca*–the more seasoned individuals have their own perfume bottles with them, and they spray themselves before the ceremony starts. Everyone then digests the plant, and not too long after, the chanting circle begins with the shaman starting first. Now I want you to focus here, because his chanting always starts by first praising the plant, and then he thanks the plant, and then he asks the plant, rocks and water for help–not all shamans are as sophisticated as this guy, but this one participates and works with the plant during the ceremony.

"He's engaging in your own personal experiences. So, while most of the tourists are lying down and thinking that this plant alone is going to heal them, that couldn't be farther from the truth. There is much more going on in the *maloca*, and, yes, a powerful shaman, if he so chooses, can participate in the healing process through sound with the spiritual dimension itself.

"This is not new knowledge. This is ancient knowledge. Remember the hieroglyphics on the walls of the ancient temples in Egypt, and how that Egyptologist was raving about the use of fragrance (essential oils and all that jazz) and its effect on human consciousness in ancient Egypt?

"Try it yourself. Take a perfume bottle you love and spray it on you. Notice how immediately you feel different and fresher. Also notice how they spray malls and stores, and how that affects your psyche and gets you in a state of receptivity. You're suddenly more relaxed and more susceptible to buy stuff. In ceremonies, it elevates your state and makes you more receptive. The juices are flowing, aren't they? What else is in play during the ceremony? You have the chanting together as a community. Sound has always been used to maintain life in traditional and indigenous cultures.

"Ultimately, the idea behind chanting is to take you away from this vicious cycle of you projecting from the past and predicting into the future. That's why it has a rhythmic pattern to it. The mind slows down enough to allow itself to let go of control and take the backseat. As such, it begins to experience the now. That's that feeling of ecstasy that you feel during chants, which again, is the same feeling of ecstasy that you've felt during those fleeting moments where you caught yourself in deep states of mediation, and were experiencing the now. It's the same theme again: humanity has mostly lost its connection with the now.

179

"During ceremonies, you were all falling in love with your-selves and with each other as a community and rediscovering the ecstasy of being completely in the now, in the present. And redis-covering the joy of being together and being in unity. You've come to conclude that truly you're most fulfilled when you're in unity with something, and you're most sad when you're separated from something. During the ceremonies, sound allowed you to overcome this state of separation—the egoic I, my, me—while you're chanting together. Through the chanting you were dissolving the boundaries between each of you and all that there is."

CHAPTER 28

THE REMEDY IS UNIVERSAL

The voice then said, "We talked about how information has been compartmentalized and then labeled as separate, as different from other information, whether labeled as scientific, spiritual, religious or otherwise. This labeling isolates; it makes it much harder for you to understand and see the truth and how it's all connected in its totality. It's important to be open and allow information to come through, so that you can finally and truly see what's going on under the hood, so to speak.

"For the past twenty-seven days here in the jungle, you've been fasting, you've been meditating, participating in group chanting, and you've seen how much control you've gained over your mind. Where else do you see the teachings of fasting? Where else do you see the use of burning incense and chanting together in a group? Yes, you used to go to church every Sunday, and those practices are not so different from what you were taught when you were younger. All of it is ultimately geared towards quietening the mind. Many traditions and religions (monotheistic or otherwise) adopt these practices in their own unique way.

181

"When you were in the foothills of the Himalayas studying yoga as taught in the Himalayan Yog-Vedantic Tradition, you quickly learned that yoga was not just an asana practice. You learned what being a yogi really meant. The practice of yoga also included all of what we just talked about, from meditation practices to fasting and taking care of the human vehicle, as well as participating in puja-sacred Hindu ritual that's done every morning to assist in refining one's state of consciousness.

Everyone is ultimately sharing their portion of the truth, but the truth in its totality can only be seen through all of them. As long as humanity continues to narrow their vision and stay within that shoebox that we talked about before, they'll continue to disempower themselves by limiting themselves all by themselves. Here's what I mean: remember those ants walking up your feet and legs earlier? See. Ants don't perceive the whole human, just the parts of them that affect their environment. For the ant walking up your left toe–to that ant–you are that left toe. To the ant walking up the right leg, you are that leg, and so on. So you see, each ant is speaking truth in describing the nature of you that they perceive, they're just not speaking the truth in its totality, because they simply can't see it from within their physical body.

"They can't see it from the dimension they occupy, because what they see is simply a magnified image, and, as such, they can only see a portion of the truth. Just like what you discovered from your Ayahuasca journey with that play in scale from micro to macro. You concluded that all that you see around you, right here and now, is simply a billion-fold-magnified point of view. You saw a pattern within a pattern within another pattern, and it didn't stop. The ant walking on your body isn't that different from those mini beings you saw within the pattern, that's within another pattern, that's within another one; yes, even that pattern is also within another one. It's missing the perspective of all of the above, and it can only see that magnified image, it can only see that portion of the truth.

"Now here's where it gets tricky. Some of the ants who 'figured out the truth' didn't share all of it with their friends and family. You're learning that systems are formed by information that others give you, but they're more formed by information that others are not giving you. You can see from your experience of participating in one of the organized religions for many years, participating in the tradition of yoga and Hindu rituals, exposing yourself to many ancient civilization sites, and, now, learning from this indigenous shaman in the Peruvian Amazon jungle that there is a thread of similarity if one takes away the distortion, labels, and all the extras that come with each traditions' personal human touch to the truth.

"The naked truth is that the core of all the teachings in their most basic, their very basic, form is geared towards the quieting of the mind. Yes ... the misery of man is universal, dear one ... and the remedy is also universal. Notice how the nature of existence is cyclical. Look at the sun, the moon and the seasons. This energy that presents itself when the time is right also makes itself available for everyone. Many will interpret it, depending on who they are. Which explains the many traditions. Because when man or woman speak, they speak what they believe to be true for themselves, based on what they've been exposed to within their culture medium. They speak beliefs of themselves to the world. Their beliefs affect the sort of communication that wants to come through. So there'll always be a certain state of distortion, which ends up creating different groups and dogmas and creating this sense of 'them versus us' and this sense of 'my doctor is better than yours,' when they're all receiving the same remedy.

"If man can only decouple the software (information they're receiving) from the operating system (their existing belief system), and then when they share the information, to share it as it is without any dependencies (attachments) on the operating system, then this universal understanding of one another becomes much easier–because

183

then their own beliefs don't affect the communication that is wanting to come through. There'll be no compatibility issues. Like I said before, when the information received is coming in a different format to what the existing operating system, aka belief system, is accustomed to, it might be immediately rejected and perceived as contradictory and controversial to what the individual currently believes to be true.

"By decoupling information from any dependencies on the operating system, this information becomes 'open source.' Anyone can take a look at it, and if they so wish, they can download the information and make it work on their own operating system (whichever they have). Remember when I said before not to wave flags at one another? Now you can see how pointless it is to try to push your beliefs onto another. It takes you nowhere. You're just wasting your time and energy.

"If the software is not compatible, it's not compatible. Period. The computer won't take it. So these debates are pointless. Try it out yourself. Try to take a software that works on macOS only and then attempt to run it on a Windows machine. What's going to happen? It will automatically be rejected because the software has dependencies on the operating system. It's not the actual software that's the problem, it's how the software was packaged. It was packaged using someone's propriety belief system.

"So you see the goal is to strip down all limitations and labels, especially this attachment to me, I and my. Life is simply life; it has no labels. It's not scientific. It's not spiritual. It's not religious. It's not anything. It simply is. Life. All life is sacred. It's nice when you're not in the game, because it gets easier to see it all for what it is. It gets easier to fully understand it, because you're not emotionally attached to the dramas. But here's the catch, the work that you came here to do is work within the game. This mind game. That's why you want to work with the mind and body, to be able to be conscious in every moment, meaning fully engaged with the game while being the observer all at the same time.

"The point is to understand that it's time for you to stop living life through an ant's point of view. It's time to pull out and see the entire picture. It's time to become more understanding of others, and as you do so, you begin to function as a unit. Just like that vision. You're the tool you're working with. You are the instrument itself. You can heal yourself.

"One way to remain healthy is through the use of sound. We talked about ingesting proper food, water that is alive, fasting, meditation, stretching and moving your body in a way that honors the energy that's coming through. We also talked about breathing and utilizing the great healer, oxygen, and now we're adding to the list the use of fragrances as well as another incredible frequency source, sound. Even geometrical shapes can heal you, but that's a conversation for another day.

"So, just like water, you are a recorder of frequency. You are continuously collecting information from your surroundings, and you're learning how to eliminate undesirable information from your body, to remain healthy through the use of the exercises above. Oh ... and add a cold shower into the mix. It will help you fight the grogginess of the mundane habit pattern of the body and mind. You'll understand it more from your own personal experience."

CHAPTER 29

LOOK THROUGH THE EYES OF SOURCE

The voice continued, "It's time to give poor Ayahuasca some love. Yes, Ayahuasca does play a role in all of this. Its role is to help you release the resistance that you have to all there is, to the witnessing and understanding of the bigger consciousness. Think of you being that ant and the bigger consciousness being that human body. Although the senses allow the ant to participate in this game of life, they are also its biggest filters. This is how the game is designed. With Ayahuasca, the ant was able to transcend its filters (physical senses), go beyond its physical form and see that it is merely a tiny ant. And all that it sees—in this case the toe of the human body—is merely a billion-fold-magnified image of all there is. Yes, that's what that Ayahuasca vision was teaching you. I won't dwell on that experience, we've already been over it.

"Ayahuasca made it possible for you to be attentive in your moment differently than you usually do—meaning being fully present—so you were able to have moments of brief awareness of this broader expansion of all that is. This is the state of complete effortless attention that we talked about earlier today. A state of deep quietness, well beyond thought, well beyond time.

"It essentially allowed you to transcend what I'm going to call the 'ants' point of view' and to see the entire picture, the truth in its totality.

"In plain English, Ayahuasca is a shortcut to everything we talked about today. It shuts down your mind and takes care of the 'letting go of control and releasing resistance' part on your behalf. This afternoon we talked about the walls of your shoebox, your world. You're so focused on your physicality that you don't let in information in formats different to those you're used to. You live within the walls of what you perceive to be legitimate information. The walls of your current beliefs. You have so many of these walls (beliefs) that contradict your own desire for growth that you don't let yourself realize and witness what's right in front of you. Ayahuasca helps you get those hindering beliefs temporarily out of the way.

"In your ceremonies, those electromagnetic walls (beliefs) disappear, and your shoebox gets larger and larger. Your body gets lighter and your limitations fade away. Yes, you create your limits with your own beliefs; otherwise you are limitless if you so choose to believe. What else can I say to convince you to take down your boundaries and stop limiting what you believe can be yours? There's one recurring theme with all of your Ayahuasca journeys, and that is that they all began by you 'letting go.' And just like that horse, that's how your journey begins as well. Just like your journey today started with you letting go of your need to control where you are and where you were heading on your walk.

"Now I know Ayahuasca served you well, and I hate to break it to you, but using a substance is not sustainable. In that altered state, you don't really accomplish any vibrational momentum, so there's no lasting effect, and it's part of the reason why people go back again ... and again ... and again ... and that's why what you're doing is the guaranteed way of enlightenment. This slow, steady conscious quieting of your mind and honoring and listening to what your body is telling you, is intentionally letting your vibration rise to the alignment of who you are. You then move through your day, just like you did today, by following your instincts to act and observe.

"Each one of you always had a unique and different Ayahuasca experience. To some it was pleasurable, and to others it was horrific. It boils down to those walls (beliefs) that we've talked about and how they align with your innate desires. The mix of the above generates different emotional results. Think of the lobster's desire to grow but the beliefs of its shell (mind/ego) are preventing it from growing and experiencing all that is. So you take a bunch of people who have a different mix of vibrations—and a different mix of the strength of their existing beliefs and their true desires for growth—and introduce the same substance, and you're going to have all kinds of different results, because you're dealing with all kinds of different vibrations.

"So, yeah, Ayahuasca can be a shortcut into an awareness of your true power by muting resistance and allowing you to look through the eyes of source, to show you that you are the observer observing itself. You are not separate from what you are observing. In other words, you are the video editor who's acting in the video and watching the video all at the same time. Take a deep breath in and consider these words slowly."

CHAPTER 30

COMING HOME

I contemplated what the voice had shared me. I then realized for the first time, that what I experienced and saw during my ceremonies was an awareness of all that is. I then said to myself, "Hmm ... interesting ... this awareness came from a state of deep quietness. A state beyond thought. A state of no belief. A state of freedom. Freedom to observe what is, as it is. Holy moly, this is what the voice was talking about earlier when we discussed meditation, time, thought, attentiveness and quietness. This is what he meant when he said, '... to explore anything with such depth, you need to be free ... to gift yourself the freedom to examine what it is that you are looking at with a quiet mind.'"

With a compassionate tone exuding love, the voice then said, "An invisible wave is pulling you in and calling you to come back, back to where you originally came from. Just like the salmon born in mountain streams, it ventures from fresh water (its origins) into the wide open ocean, where it learns to live, grow and survive in saltwater, before one day answering the deep inner call to come back home to the waters of its origins.

191

"While salmon is trying to make it back home, it rolls up its sleeves and gets itself ready to go against the current, facing all sorts of predators and seemingly impossible waterfalls before returning to the fresh waters of its origins. You're on a similar quest–the journey to discover the essence of your own true self. On this journey, you can't plan too definitively. I can give you an overall plan and an overall image, but don't try to have it all etched in stone because that wouldn't be interesting for you. You need to have the journey. You're wanting to know the destination. Where am I going? And I'm telling you that you're on the journey; you've just got on the train, dear one. You're going to go through many different places and many different cultures and many different environments and you're going to go on a journey of exploration.

"On this journey you might face challenges and seemingly impossible odds, but they're all designed to reveal to you that you're far more capable than you realize. Follow your energetic heart–your heart vortex–and get comfortable walking a different path to others when it calls you to do so. Don't worry; while salmon appears to be fighting against the current, in truth, it's supported by a series of undercurrents flowing in the direction of its journey home.

"We, your ancestors, are your undercurrents. We are the flea in your ear. We'll keep you moving, don't worry ... Your main challenge at this time is to learn how to handle thought manifestation. Everything is the game, and you buy into every portion of the game–this mind game. You are an unlimited being. All that you need to know is inside of you. It's your task to remember.

"Your human experience is your school, and the ultimate lesson is love. You are here to learn what love is, and how to love. Your challenge is to love yourself and to realize that you're designing experiences for your greatest need and growth.

"Humanity has been limited to listening to one radio station, one frequency, a frequency of fear and disempowerment. Because there were no other radio stations. Now you and many others are anchoring a new frequency and introducing a new radio station for humanity to listen to. A frequency of universal love, universal truth and sovereignty. You keep asking me, 'What is my purpose?' Well, it's quite simple. That's your wider purpose. You are here to get rid of the frequency of limitation, to anchor the frequency of information that will allow you to move beyond the need to be in fear, and show humanity that mental health and spiritual wealth are the new currency. Now, double check and make sure you have everything you need before the ceremony starts."

I asked him what his name was, and he said, "You can call me The MindChemist. I bust systems for a living. This system is busted now. It's time for you to create the freedom to move through life without limits. It's time to free yourself from everything you've learned up until today. No more reacting, no more following others, no more accepting beliefs that have been imposed upon you. No more complacency. No more grogginess and laziness. Time to understand the absolute truth for yourself. Time to reassess your unquestioned blind faith, your unquestioned beliefs–instilled within you using fear-based techniques. Time to question your thoughts, habits and find a way to become empowered again, find your way back to your soul, to who you truly are. Get to know you, the real you, that you've been ignoring this whole time.

"Stop suffering from myths–myths of Heaven and Hell. Stop suffering from imaginary scenarios that your untamed mind keeps on creating, like your social suffering–caring about how people see you and what they think of you. Stop creating scenarios in your head and getting your nervous system engaged and stressed, and limiting your experience, when none of it is real. Get it all out of your belief system. It's time for you to carry a banner of freedom that says 'I follow no one but my inner guidance.' You are up and awake. Now your challenge is to stay up. Stay awake. Stay engaged. Stay focused.

Stay alert," the voice ended firmly.

I asked him if it was possible for someone to go back to sleep after waking up.

"Of course it is," he replied. "You've had days when you woke up in the morning and then you hit the snooze button, didn't you? And sometimes you would hit the snooze button a few times before waking up again. Other times, you just went back into deep sleep after hitting snooze. Again, you already knew the answer to that question before you asked me. But I'll give you a heads up: there'll be fluctuations, and these fluctuations you'll experience are normal. Do not judge yourself for them. Sometimes abruptly fully waking up after an extremely long deep sleep can cause dis-ease.

"In fact, remember your visit to that prison in Honduras? One form of torture was to put the prisoners in a dark room for days and then expose their eyes, while keeping their eye lids forced open, to direct sunlight, and so render those prisoners blind. So take it slowly. It's the same process of working with the mind (software updates) and body (hardware resources). That sunlight is very similar to that software update; the body needs to have the capacity to handle it. Step by step, slowly but surely, you'll begin to see things differently, and one day, you'll find that you're fully up, and your eyes have adjusted to the sunlight. When that happens, don't hit snooze. Do not go back to sleep. Remain a keeper of frequency."

The voice then asked me, "How do you feel now? Do you feel any different since I tuned into you earlier this morning?"

"A piece of me feels that this is all a dream," I responded in awe. "I realize now what you've been telling me all day. It's true. Deep down, I did have all the answers to all the questions that were keeping my mind racing and my nervous system engaged. This whole time I've been running around and looking outside of me for answers when it was all inside of me. It turns out I don't need to know the why or the how behind all of it. I'm to use my heart to go through my experience. Because the heart is neutral, balanced, and can feel before the mind can understand.

"I've been laser focused on rationalizing and analyzing everything around me so that I could 'understand it' that I made little to no room for my feelings to speak. But now I know that feelings are the way to go through this reality. Now I know that accumulated knowledge in and of itself is not wisdom. Wisdom is to be felt, and lies in the silence of the physical senses ..."

After a pause I then said, "My perspective of what it entails to be a wise person has changed. A wise person is childlike and is armed with a cheeky sense of humor. Highly inquisitive. They use their childlike curiosity to see the world as beautiful. To see this life as a game and to trust enough to play with it. Why? Because they have the ability to rise above the situation they are enacting and gain a different view. A wider view from above. Yes, their power comes from the perspective that climbing above brings to them. The latter allows them to smile and laugh in the face of hardship and move forward with ease, instead of clinging to the past.

"I now understand and acknowledge that all eyes do not see with the same vision; and that there is truth in all perspectives. It's the same truth at the end of the day, but the perspective of that truth changes depending on where one is looking from. And I in my body, can only share the part of the truth that I've seen ... I can't explain the whole thing.

"What else did I learn ... oh yes. I also noticed that the more aware I become, the humbler I get, and the more I understand that I do not need to think too much of myself. Which makes it easier for my ego to accept that I do not know much. There is however, one thing I do know, and that is that all the answers I sought and the ones I still seek lie inside of me and come to me from a place of complete and utter silence.

"The hardest pill to swallow–there were a few–but the hardest one was to accept that both my happiness and my misery come from within. Many times, it seemed as if my misery was a cause from outside, but really it was lack of balance within my own mind that brought about thoughts that did not serve me ... It truly is all a big mind game; and the type of mind I carry creates my reality.

"I also learned that when one quiets their mind, then one could clearly see that the person in front of them is them. And in that person, this actor, one can find a reflection of their own nature. It just clicked in my head ... this explains what you meant when you said to me 'you can't be fully in love with yourself if you have no love for other portions of you, aka other humans.' Others are me from another perspective ... ha! At this point I also acknowledge that unless the truth is experienced, it can appear to be crooked at an intellectual level. That's where the heart comes in. The heart sees beyond the illusion and lives in the moment. In the midst of what seem to be storms in life, this still and centered voice within the heart remains clear. It is true that there are teachers outside of me but there is one true teacher and that is the teacher within."

The voice silently yet vibrationally smiled. I could feel his pride in that I was able to grasp most of what he had shared me throughout the day.

I walked inside the *maloca* and found my mat. I set my water bottle aside and sat down. I then said "Hmm ... I am here to understand and master myself ... It turned out to be much simpler than what I originally thought it was. With this clarity, I feel empowered. I now know that I can't blame anyone else for the world I find myself in, because now I'm able to flip into the station of the world that I want to experience, because now I know it's a game of frequency. All I need to do is turn the dial to the frequency I desire to experience," I said with an open heart and uplifted spirit.

After a few moments of silence, the voice said, "Your *mapacho* (tobacco) is on the other side of the *maloca*. Go get it before ceremony starts." I fetched the *mapacho*, came back to my mat and closed my eyes in preparation for the ceremony.

The voice presented itself one last time before the ceremony started and said, "Joy and abundance await you. Now that you are informed, you have no excuses. Attach your wings and fly.

"Remember, freedom is your number one priority. You are sovereign upon yourself. You are no longer this poor little stranger and afraid. Step into the knowing, and not the thinking, that without a shadow of doubt, you can have whatever it is that you want and all the abundance that you seek. Examine and choose what you want. Put energy into it. And don't worry about making a change. It's time to pierce the thin veil of doubt and uncertainty that keeps you stuck in your place. With this new clarity, pick yourself up, dust yourself off and go. You are on time.

"Now you see that the future is nothing but a child of the now. It all starts now. And now is the time for you to do what that human-like being was doing in that vision of yours. It's time to fall in love with yourself and begin to express yourself authentically, dance and spread this joy. Do not look back, or even be concerned with the old. It's time to say goodbye to all the stories you've been told. Again, it's time to free your mind and step into the knowing. Not the thinking. Step into the knowing! Know that you are protected. Know that you will be safe. With that knowing, be the fool. The fool that knows that they can have whatever they want. Just go for it. Just do it. Be very clear as to what you want, and don't worry about it. It's already yours. It's the worrying that stops it from coming to you.

"Walk in the direction that you know is right for you. Become your own authority. Bust down the boundaries that have been imposed upon you. Question everything you've been told. You are always hearing what someone else believes to be true. Stop collecting information from others. Stop accepting what others tell you. Yes, including me. Simply look at it and learn from it if you so wish. But build your own information. Build your own truth. If you simply accept what others have figured out, and what others have learned, then you'll be creating more of what others want you to create. Freedom is being responsible for your own reality. To learn about yourself from somebody else is naive. Why be a second-hand human? Discover for yourself.

"Most importantly, remember that you created all of this to play. This is a game. You're learning how to play with it. You're opening your mind and attempting to understand something bigger. When you're attempting to understand something bigger, you might feel that you're going through the crazies. Don't label and judge the experience. Just go through the experience inquisitively. Don't take anything too seriously. Nothing is as solid as you might think.

"As you tap into this new state of being, don't fight the old. Love it and thank it. Don't go through the same scenario of saying 'them versus us.' You are both the old and the new. Learn to accept and embrace both sides of you. From there, spread the light (information) and let it be known that you are all connected and what one does affects the other. Broadcast this knowing and spread this frequency for all to enjoy, just like the color spreading in that vision. This is how you serve the world you occupy."

That was when the shaman walked into the *maloca* and the ceremony started.

Made in the USA
Coppell, TX
13 December 2020

44540490R00118